LEWIS CARROLL

LEWIS CARROLL

Selected Poems

*Edited with an Introduction
by Keith Silver*

Fyfield*Books*

To N

First published in Great Britain in 1995 by
Carcanet Press Limited
Conavon Court
12-16 Blackfriars Street
Manchester M3 5BQ
Selection and introduction copyright © 1995 Keith Silver

A CIP catalogue record for this book
is available from the British Library.
ISBN 1 85754 147 2

The publisher acknowledges financial assistance
from the Arts Council of England.

Set in 10pt Palatino by Bryan Williamson, Frome
Printed and bound in England by SRP Ltd, Exeter

Contents

Illustrations

Select Bibliography

The fictional writings of Lewis Carroll are widely available, help-fully condensed into the Nonesuch Press *Complete Works of Lewis Carroll* (1939), still selling in hardback, and a chunky Penguin paperback version (1982). Both volumes include comprehensive, if rather cramped, sections devoted to the verse. While most of the 'classic' imprints produce editions of the two Alice books, other Carroll texts including *The Humorous Verse of Lewis Carroll* (1960) and the illustrated facsimile of *Alice's Adventures Underground* (1965), have been issued in separate volumes by Dover. Dover's edition of the first *Sylvie and Bruno* novel (1988) is enhanced by an introduction by Martin Gardner, whose pains-takingly researched *The Annotated Alice* (Penguin, 1964) and *The Annotated Snark* (Penguin, 1967) effectively combine the profes-sionally serious and playful elements of Carroll scholarship.

In the same spirit, William Empson's essay '*Alice in Wonderland* – The Child as Swain', in *Some Versions of Pastoral* (Chatto & Win-dus, 1935), is exhilaratingly resourceful. Other useful criticism is to be found in Walter de la Mare's *Lewis Carroll* (Cambridge, 1930), Juliet Dusinbere's *Alice to the Lighthouse* (Macmillan, 1987), and *Aspects of Alice* ed. Robert Phillips (Penguin, 1974). A more recent symposium, edited by Harold Bloom, is published by Chelsea House in their *Modern Critical Views* series.

The only biography of Carroll now easily obtainable is Derek Hudson's conscientious *Lewis Carroll – An Illustrated Biography* (Constable, 1954; illustrated edition, 1976). Hudson's enlarged format enables him to emphasize the neglected visual elements of Carroll's work, both as illustrator and photographer. There is also a brief chapter devoted to Lewis Carroll as a poet. Under-lying this volume, and well worth tracking down, are S.D. Collingwood's *The Life and Letters of Lewis Carroll* (Unwin, 1898) – a huge undertaking rushed out in the year of its subject's death – and *The Story of Lewis Carroll* (J.M. Dent, 1899) by Isa Bowman, the tomboyish Sandown bather remembered in the dedication to the Snark.

Introduction

I

Charles Lutwidge Dodgson was born at Daresbury, Cheshire, on 27 January 1832, the third child and eldest son of the Revd Charles Dodgson and Frances Jane Lutwidge. Dodgson senior was a solid Victorian divine from a family with a distinguished tradition of ecclesiastical service, a classical scholar with a reputation for paternal generosity and gifted with an unexpectedly vivid sense of humour. Mrs Dodgson is cast in the familiar nineteenth-century guise of the saintly wife and mother, content to bear her husband's children and keep his house until she died, worn out, at the age of forty-seven. S.D. Collingwood, her son's biographer, pays her fulsome tribute as 'one of the sweetest and gentlest women that ever lived, whom to know was to love'. While Dodgson undoubtedly strove to emulate his father, it was his mother's mild presence, inspiring love rather than awe, which helped to fix so decisively the memory of a secluded country childhood, 'where even the passing of a cart was a matter of great interest to the children'. Now situated in a suburb of Warrington, it is hard to imagine the remoteness of the house recalled in an affectionate poem from 1860:

> An island-farm, mid seas of corn
> Swayed by the wandering breath of morn,
> The happy spot where I was born
> ('Faces in the Fire')

With the exception of the last child, all of the Dodgson family – seven girls and four boys – were born at Daresbury. The island-farm was rapidly becoming over-populated and the Revd Dodgson's limited resources fell under a considerable strain. The spell of domestic security might easily have been broken, but in 1843 the comfortable living of Croft in north Yorkshire became vacant. Following the recommendation of Frances Egerton, a local landowner and canal magnate whose employees had benefited from Revd Dodgson's pastoral care, there arrived at Daresbury parsonage a personal letter from the Prime Minister, Robert Peel.

Flattered, gratified and relieved, the new Rector of Croft moved his family to a substantial Georgian house which he considered sturdy but without beauty. His children were perhaps more impressed. Charles came to celebrate the house in his parody of Macaulay, 'Lays of Sorrow No 2', with a suitably grand illustration of an imposing, square-faced building, replete with imaginary chimneys and windows. In its mighty shadow he began to emerge as the leader and deviser of the young Dodgsons' games. One of the most elaborate, the Railway Game, was enacted on the front lawn and involved sisters and brothers shuttling from station to station, taking refreshments and being 'upset', in which case it was 'requisite that at least 3 trains should go over them, to entitle them to the attention of the doctor and assistants'. The same ingenuity was soon being poured into a series of family magazines. Charles was largely responsible for writing, editing and illustrating three of these. The first, *Useful and Instructive Poetry* is a witty parody of schoolroom didacticism, verses culminating – like the conversation of Alice's Duchess – in a series of incongruous morals. *The Rectory Umbrella* was more varied and accomplished and contains much of the best Carroll juvenilia. Finally the scrapbook, appropriately titled *Mischmasch*, was compiled by Dodgson during his first term at Oxford and represents the parthian shot of his childhood.

By comparison, Dodgson's formal education was quiet and conventional. He worked well and diligently at Richmond Grammar School, where he excelled at Mathematics, and managed to avoid being sidetracked at Rugby, suffering the usual torments reserved for unassumingly intelligent boys no good at cricket. Despite these privations Dodgson remained emotionally absorbed in the idyllic homelife of Croft. He matriculated at Christ Church College, Oxford in May 1850, going into residence as a commoner at the beginning of the following year. Then, when he was nineteen, his mother died suddenly and the Croft epoch and childhood were over.

Escaping from grief, Dodgson threw himself with characteristic fastidiousness into the details of his life as an undergraduate. Sensitive and hardworking, he was also rather quiet, owing partly to the hereditary stammer which he tried to cure via a number of ingenious and expensive methods throughout his life, never with complete success. As tractarians gave way to liberal reformers he remained untouched by religious controversy, retaining a lifelong doctrinal moderation with a few winning idiosyncrasies; he was never able to bring himself to believe in the existence of hell. While the humour that lurked beneath his meticulous habits continued to find vent in shrewdly observed letters home – a skirmish between six dogs and their masters in Christ Church quad is untangled with ironic precision – this was offset by a disturbing strain of loss and melancholy. At twenty-one he was writing,

> I'd give all the wealth that years have piled
> the slow result of life's decay
> To be once more a little child
> For one bright summer day
> ('Solitude')

Still, he persevered at his studies with great discipline and achieved a second in classical moderations and a first in Mathematics at the end of 1852. This was rapidly followed by nomination for a studentship of Christ Church (the equivalent of a Fellowship at other colleges) by his father's friend, Dr E.B. Pusey. Pusey was at pains to assure Revd Dodgson that no personal bias had coloured his decision. Charles had certainly deserved the award, which was dependent upon his remaining unmarried and eventually proceeding to Holy Orders. With his deep-seated need for security and a systematic way of life, Dodgson was to fulfil both of these criteria and duly remained a Student of Christ Church for the rest of his days.

While Dodgson worked hard to overcome his shyness, he found lecturing and teaching traumatic; it is probable that an experiment taking classes at St Aldate's Grammar School contributed to his growing disapproval of young boys. The greater intimacy of personal tutorials proved to be more congenial. At this time he received some encouragement on the literary front, his serious poem 'Solitude' appearing in a new monthly called *The Train*, under the pseudonym 'BB'. While Dodgson had dismissed the first issue of *The Train* as largely derivative of Dickens, he was obviously gratified. When Edmund Yates, the editor, asked him to provide a fuller nom-de-plume for future contributions he was offered four alternatives:

1. *Edgar Cuthwellis* (made by transposition out of 'Charles Lutwidge'). 2. *Edgar U.C. Westhill* (ditto). 3. *Louis Carroll* (derived from Lutwidge...Ludovic...Louis, and Charles). 4. *Lewis Carroll* (ditto).

Oddly, the most accomplished submission to *The Train* – 'Upon The Lonely Moor', a parody of Wordsworth's 'Resolution and Independence' and the basis for 'The White Knight's Ballad' in *Alice Through the Looking-Glass* – did not bear the name of Lewis Carroll. This was reserved for future glory while Dodgson read the English poets, visited the theatre and pursued the new art of photography. In 1856 he spent well over £15 on camera, hood and tripod, reasoning that 'It is my one recreation and I think it should be done well.'

Among these burgeoning interests there was apparently no room for romance. Dodgson's sexuality or the absence of it has provided scope for endless speculations; despite a rumoured attachment to Ellen Terry, whom he first saw around this time, making her stage début as a child actress at the Princess's theatre, he appears never to have had any entanglements. Several missing volumes of his diary make this impossible to prove, but it seems certain that his shyness and stammer caused him severe difficulties. He was, however, already beginning to realize that he was happiest in the company of children, and especially little girls. Throughout his life the practice of photography was to provide plenty of opportunities to indulge this inclination.

It was while assembling his complicated equipment in the Deanery garden at Christ Church that Dodgson first encountered the young daughters of Dean Liddell: Ina (Lorina), Alice and Edith. 'I mark this day with a white stone', he wrote in his diary afterwards. It was not long before he was focusing his attentions and his camera on all three girls – to such an extent that Mrs Liddell became increasingly suspicious of his charms or his motives, and almost certainly jealous. This ambiguous hostility did not prevent an escape from the watchful eye of the children's governess, Mrs Prickett, one 'golden afternoon' when Dodgson, with his fellow clergyman Robinson Duckworth, rowed Ina, Alice and Edith up the Thames to Godstow. In fact the Met Office record for 4 July 1862 states that the weather in Oxford was 'cool and rather wet', despite the extraordinary concurrence among everyone in the party that it was blazing summer.[1] It is satisfying to think that when Dodgson, rowing bow, extemporized what were to become the opening chapters of *Alice's Adventures in Wonderland*, he created something like a mass hallucination.

While it is possible that Dodgson may have improvised a short rhyme like 'Twinkle, twinkle, little bat!' on the Thames, many of the poems from *Alice* already existed in one form or another before that celebrated expedition, most of the longer pieces too formally consistent to have been called spontaneously into existence. After that inspired afternoon of storytelling, the tale was augmented and enlarged in the same methodical fashion. Owing to Dodgson's exacting habits, the problem of finding a publisher and an illustrator, and the parallel enterprise of a separate hand-written version to be presented as a gift to Alice Liddell, the book did not appear until November 1865.

The reputation of Lewis Carroll and *Alice's Adventures in Wonderland* spread gradually, by word of mouth, until Queen Victoria was known to be an admirer. An apocryphal story runs that the enthusiastic sovereign asked to see the author's next work, being rather surprised to receive the *Condensation of Determinants* (1866). Indeed the industrious Dodgson published numerous mathematical works, the most accessible of which is perhaps *Euclid and his Modern Rivals* (1879). His later edition of *Euclid I and II* (1882) was of considerable contemporary importance, although little of his mathematical work survived the geometrical revolution of this century.

It was not until, after a good deal of persuasion, Dodgson managed to secure John Tenniel's services as illustrator once more, that he embarked on a sequel to Alice. This time composition was a more characteristically systematic affair. Dodgson

---

[1] See Derek Hudson, *Lewis Carroll – An Illustrated Biography* (London: Constable, 1954), Chapter 7.

searched his files again, lighting on 'Upon the Lonely Moor' and a discarded 'Stanza of Anglo-Saxon Poetry' which, with slightly modified spelling, was to become the opening refrain of 'Jabberwocky'. For the book's structure he drew more extensively on chess than he had done on cards in the first story, taking as his starting point a tale invented for the amusement of the young Liddells when they were all eagerly learning to play the game. The volume's central idea was probably suggested by a cousin named (appropriately) Alice Raikes, whom Dodgson had teasingly asked why an orange held in her right hand should appear in her left when viewed in a mirror. 'If I was on the other side of the glass,' she had replied, 'wouldn't the orange still be in my right hand?' *Alice Through the Looking Glass* was published by Macmillan's in 1871.

While he was embellishing his story books with revised versions of his old verses, Dodgson had gathered together a selection of some of his more straightforwardly ironical pieces in *Phantasmagoria* (1868), taking its title from the long opening poem which describes the inept visitation of an apprentice ghost. Among the volume's more pointed moments is 'Poeta Fit, Non Nascitur', a scarifying exposé of contemporary poetic techniques. More venomous still were the occasional poems which Dodgson included in his College pamphlets, notably *A Vision of the Three T's* (1873), a protest against the building 'improvements' to Christ Church commissioned by Dean Liddell, which can have done little to improve his relations with the elder members of that family. A good example of the combination of ingenuity and childishness which marks these works is the parody of Shakespeare beginning 'Five fathoms square the belfry frowns'.

Much of the imagery from these pamphlets – for instance a preoccupation with bathing machines which were supposed to resemble the new Christ Church belfry – spilled over into the most sustained masterpiece of nonsense poetry, *The Hunting of the Snark*. While there are plenty of bitter internecine squabbles among the characters of this strange epic, their diverse occupations leading critics to interpret its plot as (among other things) some grand commentary on the behaviour of economies under capitalism, this is no simple allegory. When asked what his poem meant, Dodgson was unable to provide an answer; we are back in the realm of inspired nonsense. The last line, 'For the Snark *was* a Boojum you see', came into his mind quite unexpectedly as he was walking in Guildford in July 1874. The rest of the poem, working more or less backwards, was put together 'at odd moments during the next year or two'.

By now Dodgson was receiving a large income from his published works, although much of this was given away in a series of annual gifts to family members. After his father's death in 1868 he had purchased a house for his unmarried sisters in Guildford known as 'The Chestnuts'. For his own part he lived modestly, subsisting on a regime of vigorous walks and biscuits and sherry, working ever harder at his numerous projects and pastimes. Then in 1881, without much regret, he resigned his lectureship, intending to devote the remainder of his life to 'worthy work in writing'. In the event he soon grew restless, upbraiding himself on the selfishness of his reclusive lifestyle. To remedy this situation he accepted the post of Curator of the Senior Common Room in the following year. For the next decade Dodgson plunged himself remorselessly into the administrative flux of college life, issuing circulars, battling with tradesmen and generally squandering his creative energies on the upkeep of the Christ Church wine cellar and terse strictures on the consistency of the Steward's mashed potatoes.

By the time Dodgson finally found the leisure to set about his 'worthy work', he discovered that the years of preoccupation had left him with a series of disjointed fragments. *Sylvie and Bruno* (1889) and its counterpart *Sylvie and Bruno Concluded* (1893), expanded from a short story originally published in the 1860s, contain a mass of disparate material, passages of charm and ingenuity frequently succeeded by a saccharine moralizing which reveals the author's writing to have come full circle. A brilliant curiosity, the whole work represents a monumental act of will.

Dodgson's life now moved in a fixed pattern between Oxford and Guildford and one of the fashionable seaside watering places, first Sandown on the Isle of Wight, then from 1877 until his death, Eastbourne. Here he would systematically set about befriending little girls, taking care always to carry a stock of safety pins to secure the hems of small paddlers. For all the wry humour of his letters, these friendships sometimes developed a precocious intensity. There is a cool, Don Juan-like efficiency about Dodgson's later liaisons, aware of their own requirements and of the inevitable conclusion that must wait upon the girl's adolescence, which is sometimes unnerving. At about this time, in line with artistic fashion, Dodgson became interested in photographing girls in the nude. Although there is no evidence that such exercises were anything other than aesthetic, and the photographer was always scrupulously careful to gain the consent of the child's parents beforehand, it seems probable that a general disapproval of this practice eventually led him to abandon his lifelong interest in photography.

This sad renunciation was symptomatic of a growing insularity towards the end of Dodgson's life. Once an ardent pursuer of celebrities himself, the avoidance of personal publicity now became something of a mania. Throughout the 1870s and the early 1880s, as publicity itself moved towards its twentieth century maturity, the ascendant fame of Lewis Carroll meant that a stream of admirers had begun to find their way to Christ Church. Dodgson responded in characteristic fashion, producing a flyer in which he, Charles Lutwidge Dodgson, formally disclaimed any connection whatsoever with the said Lewis Carroll and his published works. Of course, all this really proved was that his appetite for print was as vital as it always had been. His last work, 'Symbolic Logic', was only half complete when in 1897, suffering from exhaustion, he contracted bronchial symptoms and like the 'older children' in the dedicatory poem of *Through the Looking-Glass*, went to bed forever.

II

The early poems which we now attribute to Lewis Carroll were written for the amusement of the captive audience at Croft. Appearing in a series of family magazines, most notably *Useful and Instructive Poetry*, *The Rectory Umbrella* and the Oxford scrap book *Mischmasch*, they derive much of their humour from taking impish pot-shots at the impregnable domestic life of the Dodgson family. The Useful and Instructive poems in particular, with their mockery of copy book maxims – 'You mustn't', 'Never stew your sister', 'Behave' – by their very playfulness reinforce the order of the family home. Similarly the tendency towards comic brutality already manifest in them – a troublesome brother is used as live bait on a fishhook in the Tees; a stranger, perhaps an intruder on the country isolation of Croft, is run through with a golden pin – serves to reinforce the inviolable safety of 'here'. Grotesque horrors are effectively contained by the formal patterns of the verse.

Throughout Carroll's *oeuvre* there is a profusion of words emphasized by italics, a habit which seems to have been partly acquired from Mrs Dodgson whose letters employ the same insistent technique. The early poems make extensive use of this method, often to pitch an imitation of some nuance of contemporary speech; Carroll has a fine, if limited dramatic ear. As frequently, italic emphasis is used to create a mock heroic effect, in the traditional sense, as in the splendid parody of Macaulay which deals with the efforts of the Dodgson children to goad an obdurate donkey up the Dalton road, but also to approximate a childish apprehension of vastness – ''Twould *never* reach the *nearest* star,/Because it is so *very* far' ('Facts'). This seems to reflect a kind of deliberate English parochialism in the face of huge grown up realities, the empire and global power. A keynote in all Carroll's work is this very knowing compression of realities.

Of course the other principal use of italics here is to point out the rigorously specific – '*That* shows a punctual mind', a finickety fervour which was to reach its apotheosis with the moralizing Duchess in *Alice's Adventures in Wonderland*. Throughout his life Carroll loved particulars for their own sake and was aware of how good sense, reduced to its specifics, could become absurd. This perhaps accounts for the relish he found in the tradition of sober instruction parodied in *Useful and Instructive Poetry*. Like Blake, the flights of his early imagination were launched from the common sense base of improving literature.

Perhaps the wildest of all these flights, 'Jabberwocky', curiously recalls Blake's 'The Tyger' with its concluding repetition of a powerful first stanza and pervasive atmosphere of awe and menace. It is strange that, although the Jabberwocky is summarily despatched, the poem loses none of its pregnancy. Partly because of the closing reprise the piece seems unresolved, its menace reaffirmed. It is as though the hero has overcome the burbling monster too easily, almost in obedience to a ritual pattern. There is no extra stanza to lend a blood-and-guts reality to the fatal snicker-snack of the vorpal blade. The wood, which may well still be full of worse horrors – Jubjub birds, Bandersnatches, or even Boojums – retains a primaeval integrity. The whole poem is like some pagan drama of man's hard-won mastery over nature. When the hero meditates under the Tumtum tree, he is like Buddha under the Bo tree.

The Jabberwocky, like the other fabulous animals in Carroll, was possibly given some currency by recent discoveries in Natural History and by the Darwin controversy, *The Origin of Species* having appeared just seven years before the first Alice volume in 1859. The creature is certainly a vivid embodiment of Tennyson's comment on a new, ruthless 'Nature, red in tooth and claw'. Tenniel's well-known illustration endows the beast with a pair of the most formidable claws, although the teeth have, one supposes, been toned down in deference to anxious mothers. Such delicacy is conspicuously absent from Carroll's brutal nonsense world where brother stews sister, Walrus and Carpenter feast on talking oysters and Panther rudely devours Owl. This viciousness is not, however, the full story.

The whole evolution debate in the mid-nineteenth century came at the end of a period of mounting anxiety about the apparent cruelty of Nature and God. Fossilized bones could no longer be dismissed as geological freaks or as the remains of elephants imported by the Romans. It became gradually clear that they represented countless species which the Creator had inexplicably permitted to become extinct. 'From scarpèd cliff and quarried stone,' says Tennyson, 'She cries, "A thousand types are gone:/ I care for nothing, all shall go."' These lines, together with the famous phrase, come from *In Memoriam*, a poem which an admiring Dodgson and his sisters had taken it upon themselves to index. We know that Dodgson was gratified when Tennyson, in return, displayed a keen interest in some of his anatomical photographs, 'especially a group of human skeletons and a monkey'. Undoubtedly he would at some time have considered the chilling suspicion that, since so many other species had peremptorily expired, was it not possible that we too might one day 'softly and suddenly' vanish away?

In this light Carroll's *The Hunting of the Snark*, with its abrupt and arresting denouement, might be read as a dramatic account of the human race's new apprehension of the possibility of its own extinction. Of course, this many-faceted work has been, can be and will be interpreted in a bewildering variety of ways; this approach is simply a backdated version of Martin Gardiner's apocalyptic 1962 commentary, written in the shadow of the Cuban missile crisis.[2] Evolutionary clues to the Baker's final chilling disappearance may be discerned in the Snark's own fabulous nature – another curious living fossil – or in Carroll's penchant for backward movement, the direction in which both the hunter's ship and the poet's imagination regressed.

There are evolutionary hints elsewhere in Carroll's work. The author identifies himself with the ungainly and anachronistic Dodo in *Alice's Adventures in Wonderland*, its name a stuttering approximation of DoDoDodgson. William Empson has also drawn attention to the emergence of the animals from the primaeval pool of tears, taking the caucus race to represent natural selection.[3] Here Alice's human supremacy is finally conferred by the gift of the thimble. It may be significant that the intrepid Snark hunters, besides being armed with railway shares, forks, hope and the rest, primarily 'sought it with thimbles'. Since Carroll has infected us with the moralizing habit it becomes tempting to conclude that the Baker's fate signifies that human superiority can no longer be complacently sustained. When the Butcher and the Beaver overcome what was generally thought to be a natural antipathy in Fit the Fifth, their loving friendship perhaps expresses a new and unavoidable interconnectedness between man

---

[2] Lewis Carroll, *The Annotated Snark*, ed. Martin Gardiner (Penguin Books, 1967).

[3] William Empson, '*Alice in Wonderland* – The Child as Swain', *Some Versions of Pastoral* (London: Hogarth Press, 1935).

and animal, hunter and hunted. After all, it's easy to confuse 'Snark' with 'Ark', and the ship contains a fairly representative cross-section of human types, the doomed Baker murmuring in 'anti-diluvian' tones.

Also outmoded are the old kind of heroics. Against the mysterious curse of the Boojum one cannot begin to struggle. The Jabberwocky seems to have been slain long ago in its own elliptical never-never. The White Knight in *Through the Looking-Glass* is heroic, but in a new way. It is his self-appointed task to get to grips with the unassimilable pluralities of the modern world. His permanently mesmerized state is like a wound sustained in battle. When the Carroll of 'Jabberwocky' or the *Snark* uses portmanteau words, straining to pack together several disparate meanings with an implied aspiration towards spontaneous revelation, he is, I believe, doing something akin to the White Knight, relentlessly slinging 'useful' objects over the back of his hapless charger. The tragedy is that the White Knight, pursuing truth through the accumulation of particulars, has only succeeded in creating his own isolated world. His literary equivalent would be *Finnegans Wake*. Nonsense here becomes the antithesis of common sense – his discourse is logical but individualistic, esoteric, eccentric. He is unable to hold a conversation with the 'aged, aged man' who is 'saved' by his poverty and the demands of daily survival, trying to touch his aristocratic interrogator for a drink. It is only when this important request is made that the Knight finally hears, although he fails to understand. The class difference serves to emphasize the absence of any common culture.

The White Knight has a scientific mind and is the epitome of detachment. He is proud of the fact that he has 'Invented a new pudding during the main course', thus signifying a triumph of the intellect over the sense. Nonsense here means non-sensual. Carroll was always most comfortable with those forms of mathematical or scientific thought which demanded no complicated emotional commitment from him. Repeatedly his nonsense makes the emotions lag with comic awkwardness behind an agile logic which they cannot quite comprehend. By the same token there is much satisfaction to be gained from enjoying chaos or absurdity without having ever to relinquish a sense of implicit order. It may be that the enormous popularity of this kind of writing in the nineteenth century was partly due to its politely embodying something of the Victorian malaise, the age's ideological confusion, but with the tacit reassurance that it was all so obviously a game; we shall always wake up in the end, we shall always be home in time for tea. The rules of the game, Alice's cards or chess, remain to suggest a final impersonal order. The irony of the writing, and even the purest nonsense is ironic in its humorous distance from the norms of expression, implies an ultimate orthodoxy.

The logic under the incongruous surface takes various forms. It may mean consistently believing the opposite of what appears self-evidently true; 'you *said* I was plain and *excessively* vain,/But I knew that you *meant* I was pretty', exclaims the imperious lover in 'Ode to Damon'. With considerable dexterity the refrain of 'The Mock Turtle's Song' actually makes apparent opposites, 'Will you, won't you', mean the same thing. If occasional contradiction is not enough, a whole narrative might be reversed. Alice steps into the inverted world of the looking-glass; in *Sylvie and Bruno* time starts to run in backwards. In fact, it is possible to move so far in reverse as to complete the circle, arriving back at the number first thought of. Carroll is fascinated by the circular possibilities of the new return rail ticket which he affords the expansive scope of homeric similes in 'Lays of Sorrow No. 1' and 'Phantasmagoria'. When Alice is told to 'Take a return ticket every time the train stops' it is as though progress is turning in on itself.

Other spans of Carroll's poetic imagination, 'Father William' or 'The White Knight's Ballad', are structured via a series of enquiries. No matter how outlandish the question, the underlying logic stipulates that the answer will always be a binary 'yes' or 'no'. Order can also be created through arbitrary number games, like the famous declaration in the Snark that everything repeated three times is true. Carroll's nonsense is often a melody or hybrid of different systems. Empson observes that 'Alice is interested in conventions and wants to learn new ones', although her anxiousness to acquire them betrays a detachment from them. She and Carroll, like gifted children, are free to enjoy rules for their own sake, fabricating elaborate structures.

Verse also bestows the necessary organization with its disciplined beats, lines and stanzas and, Carroll shows, can confer plausibility on the most overtly ludicrous subject matter. A collection of Lewis Carroll's poems will embody many of the central contradictions of his writing, not least the mutually dependent relationship of order and chaoes. We belong to neither. Laughing at absurdity, it is perplexing to find that Carroll's order can be demonstrably more consistent than 'common sense' which is really pragmatic, subjective and tailored to human needs in the world. In fact, taken to its conclusion, Carroll's implacable logic may be no more comfortable than Darwin's view of nature or the Boojum-haunted wastes beyond Wonderland.

My Fairy

I have a fairy by my side
   Which says I must not sleep,
When once in pain I loudly cried
   It said 'You must not weep.'

If, full of mirth, I smile and grin,
   It says 'You must not laugh;'
When once I wished to drink some gin
   It said 'You must not quaff.'

When once a meal I wished to taste
   It said 'You must not bite;'
When to the wars I went in haste
   It said 'You must not fight.'

'What may I do?' at length I cried,
   Tired of the painful task.
The fairy quietly replied,
   And said 'You must not ask.'

Moral: 'You mustn't.'

Brother and Sister

'Sister, sister, go to bed!
Go and rest your weary head.'
Thus the prudent brother said.

'Do you want a battered hide,
Or scratches to your face applied?'
Thus his sister calm replied.

1

'Sister, do not raise my wrath.
I'd make you into mutton broth
As easily as kill a moth!'

The sister raised her beaming eye
And looked on him indignantly
And sternly answered, 'Only try!'

Off to the cook he quickly ran.
'Dear Cook, please lend a frying-pan
To me as quickly as you can.'

'And wherefore should I lend it you?'
'The reason, Cook, is plain to view.
I wish to make an Irish stew.'

'What meat is in that stew to go?'
'My sister'll be the contents!'
                              'Oh!'
'You'll lend the pan to me, Cook?'
                              'No!'

Moral: Never stew your sister.

Rules and Regulations

A short direction
To avoid dejection,
By variations
In occupations,
And prolongation
Of relaxation,
And combinations
Of recreations,
And disputation

On the state of the nation
In adaptation
To your station,
By invitations
To friends and relations,
By evitation
Of amputation,
By permutation
In conversation,
And deep reflection
You'll avoid dejection.

Learn well your grammar,
And never stammer,
Write well and neatly,
And sing most sweetly,
Be enterprising,
Love early rising,
Go walk of six miles,
Have ready quick smiles,
With lightsome laughter,
Soft flowing after.
Drink tea, not coffee;
Never eat toffy.
Eat bread with butter.
One more, don't stutter.
Don't waste your money,
Abstain from honey.
Shut doors behind you,
(Don't slam them, mind you),
Drink beer, not porter.
Don't enter the water
Till to swim you are able.
Sit close to the table.
Take care of a candle.
Shut a door by the handle,
Don't push with your shoulder
Until you are older.

Lose not a button.
Refuse cold mutton.
Starve your canaries.
Believe in fairies.
If you are able,
Don't have a stable
With any mangers.
Be rude to strangers.

Moral: Behave.

Lays of Sorrow

NO. 1

The day was wet, the rain fell souse
    Like jars of strawberry jam,[1] a
Sound was heard in the old henhouse,
    A beating of a hammer.
Of stalwart form, and visage warm,
    Two youths were seen within it,
Splitting up an old tree into perches for their poultry
    At a hundred strokes[2] a minute.

The work is done, the hen has taken
Possession of her nest and eggs,
Without a thought of eggs and bacon,[3]
(Or I am very much mistaken):
    She turns over each shell,
    To be sure that all's well,
    Looks into the straw
    To see there's no flaw,

---

[1] *I.e.* the jam with the jars. Observe the beauty of this rhyme.
[2] At the rate of a stroke and two-thirds in a second.
[3] Unless the hen was a poacher, which is unlikely.

Goes once round the house,[4]
Half afraid of a mouse,
Then sinks calmly to rest
On the top of her nest,
  First doubling up each of her legs.

Time rolled away, and so did every shell,
    'Small by degrees and beautifully less,'
As the sage mother with a powerful spell[5]
      Forced each in turn its contents to express,[6]
      But ah! 'imperfect is expression,'
      Some poet said, I don't care who,
      If you want to know you must go elsewhere,
      One fact I can tell, if you're willing to hear,
      He never attended a Parliament Session,
      For I'm certain that if he had ever been there,
      Full quickly would he have changed his ideas,
      With the hissings, the hootings, the groans and the cheers.
      And as to his name it is pretty clear
      That it wasn't me and it wasn't you!

And so it fell upon a day,
    (That is, it never rose again)
A chick was found upon the hay,
Its little life had ebbed away.
No longer frolicsome and gay,
No longer could it run or play.
'And must we, chicken, must we part?'
Its master[7] cried with bursting heart,
    And voice of agony and pain.
So one, whose ticket's marked 'Return,'[8]
When to the lonely roadside station
He flies in fear and perturbation,

---

[4] The henhouse.   [5] Beak and claw.   [6] Press out.
[7] Probably one of the two stalwart youths.
[8] The system of return tickets is an excellent one. People are conveyed, on particular days, there and back again for one fare.

Thinks of his home – the hissing urn –
Then runs with flying hat and hair,
And entering, finds to his despair
    He's missed the very latest train.[9]

Too long it were to tell of each conjecture
    Of chicken suicide, and poultry victim,
The deadly frown, the stern and dreary lecture,
    The timid guess, 'perhaps some needle pricked him!'
The din of voice, the words both loud and many,
    The sob, the tear, the sigh that none could smother,
Till all agreed 'a shilling to a penny
    It killed itself, and we acquit the mother!'
    Scarce was the verdict spoken,
    When that still calm was broken,
A childish form hath burst into the throng;
    With tears and looks of sadness,
    That bring no news of gladness,
But tell too surely something hath gone wrong!
'The sight that I have come upon
    The stoutest heart[10] would sicken,
That nasty hen has been and gone
    And killed another chicken!'

---

[9] An additional vexation would be that his 'Return' ticket would be no use the next day.
[10] Perhaps even the 'bursting' heart of its master.

Lays of Sorrow
NO. 2

Fair stands the ancient[1] Rectory,
   The Rectory of Croft,
The sun shines bright upon it,
   The breezes whisper soft.
From all the house and garden
   Its inhabitants come forth,
And muster in the road without,
And pace in twos and threes about,
   The children of the North.

Some are waiting in the garden,
   Some are waiting at the door,
And some are following behind,
   And some have gone before.
But wherefore all this mustering?
   Wherefore this vast array?
A gallant feat of horsemanship
   Will be performed to-day.

To eastward and to westward,
   The crowd divides amain,
Two youths are leading on the steed,
   Both tugging at the rein;
And sorely do they labour,
   For the steed[2] is very strong,
And backward moves its stubborn feet,
And backward ever doth retreat,
   And drags its guides along.

---

[1] This Rectory has been supposed to have been built in the time of Edward VI, but recent discoveries clearly assign its origin to a much earlier period. A stone has been found in an island formed by the river Tees on which is inscribed the letter 'A', which is justly conjectured to stand for the name of the great King Alfred, in whose reign this house was probably built.
[2] The poet entreats pardon for having represented a donkey under this dignified name.

And now the knight hath mounted,
    Before the admiring band,
Hath got the stirrups on his feet,
    The bridle in his hand.
Yet, oh! beware, sir horseman!
    And tempt thy fate no more,
For such a steed as thou hast got
    Was never rid before!

The rabbits bow before thee,
    And cower in the straw;
The chickens[3] are submissive,
    And own thy will for law;
Bullfinches and canary
    Thy bidding do obey;
And e'en the tortoise in its shell
    Doth never say thee nay.

But thy steed will hear no master,
    Thy steed will bear no stick,
And woe to those that beat her,
    And woe to those that kick![4]
For though her rider smite her,
    As hard as he can hit,
And strive to turn her from the yard,
She stands in silence, pulling hard
Against the pulling bit.

And now the road to Dalton
    Hath felt their coming tread,
The crowd are speeding on before,
    And all have gone ahead.
Yet often look they backward,
    And cheer him on, and bawl,
For slower still, and still more slow,

---

[3] A full account of the history and misfortunes of these interesting creatures may be found in the first 'Lay of Sorrow'.
[4] It is a singular fact that a donkey makes a point of returning any kicks offered to it.

That horseman and that charger go,
And scarce advance at all.

And now two roads to choose from
    Are in that rider's sight:
In front the road to Dalton,
    And New Croft upon the right.
'I can't get by!' he bellows,
    'I really am not able!
Though I pull my shoulder out of joint,
I cannot get him past this point,
    For it leads unto his stable!'

Then out spake Ulfrid Longbow,[5]
    A valiant youth was he,
'Lo! I will stand on thy right hand
    And guard the pass for thee!'
And out spake fair Flureeza,[6]
    His sister eke was she,
'I will abide on thy other side,
    And turn thy steed for thee!'

And now commenced a struggle
    Between that steed and rider,
For all the strength that he hath left
    Doth not suffice to guide her.
Though Ulfrid and his sister
    Have kindly stopped the way,
And all the crowd have cried aloud,
    'We can't wait here all day!'

Round turned he as not deigning
    Their words to understand,
But he slipped the stirrups from his feet
    The bridle from his hand,
And grasped the mane full lightly,

---

[5] This valiant knight, besides having a heart of steel and nerves of iron, has been lately in the habit of carrying a brick in his eye.
[6] She was sister to both.

9

And vaulted from his seat,
And gained the road in triumph,[7]
And stood upon his feet.

All firmly till that moment
   Had Ulfrid Longbow stood,
And faced the foe right valiantly,
   As every warrior should.
But when safe on terra firma
   His brother he did spy,
'What *did* you do that for?' he cried,
Then unconcerned he stepped aside
   And let it canter by.

They gave him bread and butter,[8]
   That was of public right,
As much as four strong rabbits
   Could munch from morn to night,
For he'd done a deed of daring,
   And faced that savage steed,
And therefore cups of coffee sweet,
And everything that was a treat,
   Were but his right and meed.

And often in the evenings,
   When the fire is blazing bright,
When books bestrew the table
   And moths obscure the light,
When crying children go to bed,
   A struggling, kicking load;
We'll talk of Ulfrid Longbow's deed,
How, in his brother's utmost need,
Back to his aid he flew with speed,
And how he faced the fiery steed,
   And kept the New Croft Road.

---

[7] The reader will probably be at a loss to discover the nature of this triumph, as no object was gained, and the donkey was obviously the victor; on this point, however, we are sorry to say we can offer no good explanation.

[8] Much more acceptable to a true knight than 'corn-land' which the Roman people were so foolish as to give to their daring champion, Horatius.

The Two Brothers

There were two brothers at Twyford school,
　　And when they had left the place,
It was, 'Will ye learn Greek and Latin?
　　Or will ye run me a race?
Or will ye go up to yonder bridge,
　　And there we will angle for dace?'

'I'm too stupid for Greek and for Latin,
　　I'm too lazy by half for a race,
So I'll even go up to yonder bridge,
　　And there we will angle for dace.'

He has fitted together two joints of his rod,
　　And to them he has added another,
And then a great hook he took from his book,
　　And ran it right into his brother.

Oh much is the noise that is made among boys
　　When playfully pelting a pig,
But a far greater pother was made by his brother
　　When flung from the top of the brigg.

The fish hurried up by the dozens,
　　All ready and eager to bite,
For the lad that he flung was so tender and young,
　　It quite gave them an appetite.

Said he, 'Thus shall he wallop about
　　And the fish take him quite at their ease,
For me to annoy it was ever his joy,
　　Now I'll teach him the meaning of "Tees"!'

The wind to his ear brought a voice,
　　'My brother, you didn't had ought ter!
And what have I done that you think it such fun
　　To indulge in the pleasure of slaughter?

'A good nibble or bite is my chiefest delight
    When I'm merely expected to *see*,
But a bite from a fish is not quite what I wish,
    When I get it performed upon *me*;
And just now here's a swarm of dace at my arm,
    And a perch has got hold of my knee.

'For water my thirst was not great at the first,
    And of fish I have quite sufficien—'
'Oh fear not!' he cried, 'for whatever betide,
    We are both in the selfsame condition!

'I am sure that our state's very nearly alike
    (Not considering the question of slaughter),
For I have my perch on the top of the bridge,
    And you have your perch in the water.

'I stick to my perch and your perch sticks to you,
    We are really extremely alike;
I've a turn-pike up here, and I very much fear
    You may soon have a turn with a pike.'

'Oh grant but one wish! If I'm took by a fish
    (For your bait is your brother, good man!)
Pull him up if you like, but I hope you will strike
    As gently as ever you can.'

'If the fish be a trout, I'm afraid there's no doubt
    I must strike him like lightning that's greased;
If the fish be a pike, I'll engage not to strike,
    Till I've waited ten minutes at least.'

'But in those ten minutes to desolate Fate
    Your brother a victim may fall!'
'I'll reduce it to five, so *perhaps* you'll survive,
    But the chance is exceedingly small.'

'Oh hard is your heart for to act such a part;
  Is it iron, or granite, or steel?'
'Why, I really can't say – it is many a day
  Since my heart was accustomed to feel.

''Twas my heart-cherished wish for to slay many fish,
  Each day did my malice grow worse,
For my heart didn't soften with doing it so often,
  But rather, I should say, the reverse.'

'Oh would I were back at Twyford school,
  Learning lessons in fear of the birch!'
'Nay, brother!' he cried, 'for whatever betide,
  You are better off here with your perch!

'I am sure you'll allow you are happier now,
  With nothing to do but to play;
And this single line here, it is perfectly clear,
  Is much better than thirty a day!

'And as to the rod hanging over your head,
  And apparently ready to fall,
That, you know, was the case, when you lived in that place,
  So it need not be reckoned at all.

'Do you see that old trout with a turn-up-nose snout?
  (Just to speak on a pleasanter theme,)
Observe, my dear brother, our love for each other –
  He's the one I like best in the stream.

'To-morrow I mean to invite him to dine
  (We shall all of us think it a treat);
If the day should be fine, I'll just *drop him a line*,
  And we'll settle what time we're to meet.

'He hasn't been into society yet,
  And his manners are not of the best,
So I think it quite fair that it should be *my* care,
  To see that he's properly dressed.'

Many words brought the wind of 'cruel' and 'kind',
   And that 'man suffers more than the brute':
Each several word with patience he heard,
   And answered with wisdom to boot.

'What? prettier swimming in the stream,
   Than lying all snugly and flat?
Do but look at that dish filled with glittering fish,
   Has Nature a picture like that?

'What? a higher delight to be drawn from the sight
   Of fish full of life and of glee?
What a noodle you are! 'tis delightfuller far
   To kill them than let them go free!

'I know there are people who prate by the hour
   Of the beauty of earth, sky, and ocean;
Of the birds as they fly, of the fish darting by,
   Rejoicing in Life and in Motion.

'As to any delight to be got from the sight,
   It is all very well for a flat,
But *I* think it all gammon, for hooking a salmon
   Is better than twenty of that!

'They say that a man of a right-thinking mind
   Will *love* the dumb creatures he sees –
What's the use of his mind, if he's never inclined
   To pull a fish out of the Tees?

'Take my friends and my home – as an outcast I'll roam:
   Take the money I have in the Bank;
It is just what I wish, but deprive me of *fish*,
   And my life would indeed be a blank!'

Forth from the house his sister came,
   Her brothers for to see,
But when she saw that sight of awe,
   The tear stood in her e'e.

'Oh what bait's that upon your hook,
   My brother, tell to me?'
'It is but the fantailed pigeon,
   He would not sing for me.'

'Whoe'er would expect a pigeon to sing,
   A simpleton he must be!
But a pigeon-cote is a different thing
   To the coat that there I see!'

'Oh what bait's that upon your hook,
   Dear brother, tell to me?'
'It is my younger brother,' he cried,
   'Oh woe and dole is me!

'I's mighty wicked, that I is!
   Or how could such things be?
Farewell, farewell, sweet sister,
   I'm going o'er the sea.'

'And when will you come back again,
   My brother, tell to me?'
'When chub is good for human food,
   And that will never be!'

She turned herself right round about,
   And her heart brake into three,
Said, 'One of the two will be wet through and through,
   And t'other'll be late for his tea!'

Dedication
to Alice's Adventures in Wonderland

All in the golden afternoon
   Full leisurely we glide;
For both our oars, with little skill,
   By little arms are plied,
While little hands make vain pretence
   Our wanderings to guide.

Ah, cruel Three! In such an hour
   Beneath such dreamy weather,
To beg a tale of breath too weak
   To stir the tiniest feather!
Yet what can one poor voice avail
   Against three tongues together?

Imperious Prima flashes forth
   Her edict 'to begin it' –
In gentler tone Secunda hopes
   'There will be nonsense in it!' –
While Tertia interrupts the tale
   Not *more* than once a minute.

Anon, to sudden silence won,
   In fancy they pursue
The dream-child moving through a land
   Of wonders wild and new,
In friendly chat with bird or beast –
   And half believe it true.

And ever, as the story drained
   The wells of fancy dry,
And faintly strove that weary one
   To put the subject by,
'The rest next time –' 'It *is* next time!'
   The happy voices cry.

Thus grew the tale of Wonderland:
    Thus slowly, one by one,
Its quaint events were hammered out –
    And now the tale is done,
And home we steer, a merry crew,
    Beneath the setting sun.

Alice! a childish story take,
    And with a gentle hand
Lay it where Childhood's dreams are twined
    In Memory's mystic band,
Like pilgrim's wither'd wreath of flowers
    Pluck'd in a far-off land.

How Doth . . .

How doth the little crocodile
    Improve his shining tail,
And pour the waters of the Nile
    On every golden scale!

How cheerfully he seems to grin,
    How neatly spreads his claws,
And welcomes little fishes in
    With gently smiling jaws!

The Mouse's Tale

Fury said to a
            mouse, That he
            met in the
        house,
    'Let us
      both go to
        law: *I* will
            prosecute
                you. Come
                    I'll take no
                    denial; We
                    must have a
                trial: For
        really this
        morning I've
    nothing
  to do.'
    Said the
        mouse to the
                cur, 'Such
                    a trial
                    dear Sir,
                        With
                    no jury
                or judge,
        would be
        wasting
    our
    breath.'
            'I'll be
                judge, I'll
                    be jury,'
                        Said
                    cunning
                old Fury:
            'I'll
            try the
                whole
                    cause,
                        and
                    condemn
                you
            to
            death.'

Father William

'You are old Father William,' the young man said,
   'And your hair has become very white;
And yet you incessantly stand on your head –
   Do you think, at your age, it is right?

'In my youth,' Father William replied to his son,
   'I feared it might injure the brain;
But, now that I'm perfectly sure I have none,
   Why, I do it again and again.'

'You are old,' said the youth, 'as I mentioned before,
   And have grown most uncommonly fat;
Yet you turned a back-somersault in at the door –
   Pray, what is the reason of that?'

'In my youth,' said the sage, as he shook his grey locks,
  'I kept all my limbs very supple
By the use of this ointment – one shilling a box –
  Allow me to sell you a couple?'

'You are old,' said the youth, 'and your jaws are too weak
  For anything tougher than suet;
Yet you finished the goose, with the bones and the beak –
  Pray, how did you manage to do it?'

'In my youth,' said his father, 'I took to the law,
  And argued each case with my wife;
And the muscular strength, which it gave to my jaw,
  Has lasted the rest of my life.'

'You are old,' said the youth, 'one would hardly suppose
  That your eye was as steady as ever;
Yet you balanced an eel on the end of your nose –
  What made you so awfully clever?'

'I have answered three questions, and that is enough,'
  Said his father; 'don't give yourself airs!
Do you think I can listen all day to such stuff?
  Be off, or I'll kick you down stairs!'

The Duchess's Lullaby

Speak roughly to your little boy,
　　And beat him when he sneezes:
He only does it to annoy,
　　Because he knows it teases.

CHORUS

Wow! wow! wow!

I speak severely to my boy,
　　I beat him when he sneezes;
For he can thoroughly enjoy
　　The pepper when he pleases!

CHORUS

Wow! wow! wow!

The Mad Hatter's Song

Twinkle, twinkle, little bat!
How I wonder what you're at!
Up above the world you fly,
Like a tea-tray in the sky.
　　　　　Twinkle, twinkle –

The Mock Turtle's Song

'Will you walk a little faster?' said a whiting to a snail.
'There's a porpoise close behind us, and he's treading on my tail.
See how eagerly the lobsters and the turtles all advance!
They are waiting on the shingle – will you come and join the
    dance?
    Will you, won't you, will you, won't you, will you join the
      dance?
    Will you, won't you, will you, won't you, won't you join the
      dance?

'You can really have no notion how delightful it will be,
When they take us up and throw us, with the lobsters, out to sea!'
But the snail replied 'Too far, too far!' and gave a look askance –
Said he thanked the whiting kindly, but he would not join the
    dance.
    Would not, could not, would not, could not, would not join
      the dance.
    Would not, could not, would not, could not, could not join
      the dance.

'What matters it how far we go?' his scaly friend replied.
'There is another shore, you know, upon the other side.
The further off from England the nearer is to France –
Then turn not pale, beloved snail, but come and join the dance.
    Will you, won't you, will you, won't you, will you join the
      dance?
    Will you, won't you, will you, won't you, won't you join the
      dance?

Alice's Recitation

'Tis the voice of the Lobster; I heard him declare,
'You have baked me too brown, I must sugar my hair.'
As a duck with its eyelids, so he with his nose
Trims his belt and his buttons, and turns out his toes.
When the sands are all dry, he is gay as a lark,
And will talk in contemptuous tones of the Shark:
But, when the tide rises and sharks are around,
His voice has a timid and tremulous sound.

I passed by his garden, and marked, with one eye,
How the Owl and the Panther were sharing a pie:
The Panther took the pie-crust, and gravy, and meat,
While the Owl had the dish as its share of the treat.[1]
When the pie was all finished, the Owl, as a boon,
Was kindly permitted to pocket the spoon:
While the Panther received knife and fork with a growl,
And concluded the banquet by —

Later concluded by the author thus:

But the Panther obtained both the fork and the knife,
So, when *he* lost his temper, the Owl lost its life.

---

[1] Dodgson later adapted this poem for a musical setting by William Boyd. Here the second stanza reads:

> I passed by his garden, and marked, with one eye,
> How the owl and the oyster were sharing a pie;
> While the duck and the Dodo, the lizard and cat
> Were swimming in milk round the brim of a hat.

Dodgson maintained a keen interest in the various theatrical presentations of his work. The 'standard' version of this poem, printed above, was expanded from its six-line nucleus to meet the requirements of Savile Clarke's musical production of *Alice in Wonderland* at the Prince of Wales' Theatre in 1886. It has appeared in this form in all subsequent editions of the book. – *Ed.*

Turtle Soup

Beautiful Soup, so rich and green,
Waiting in a hot tureen!
Who for such dainties would not stoop?
Soup of the evening, beautiful Soup!
Soup of the evening, beautiful Soup!
    Beau–ootiful Soo–oop!
    Beau–ootiful Soo–oop!
Soo—oop of the e—e—evening,
    Beautiful, beautiful Soup!

Beautiful Soup! Who cares for fish,
Game, or any other dish?
Who would not give all else for two p
ennyworth only of beautiful Soup?
Pennyworth only of beautiful Soup?
    Beau—ootiful Soo—oop!
    Beau—ootiful Soo—oop!
Soo—oop of the e—e—evening,
    Beautiful, beauti—FUL SOUP!

Evidence Read at the Trial of Knave of Hearts

They told me you had been to her,
    And mentioned me to him:
She gave me a good character,
    But said I could not swim.

He sent them word I had not gone,
   (We know it to be true):
If she should push the matter on,
   What would become of you?

I gave her one, they gave him two,
   You gave us three or more;
They all returned from him to you,
   Though they were mine before.

If I or she should chance to be
   Involved in this affair,
He trusts to you to set them free,
   Exactly as we were.

My notion was that you had been
   (Before she had this fit)
An obstacle that came between
   Him, and ourselves, and it.

Don't let him know she liked them best,
   For this must ever be
A secret kept from all the rest,
   Between yourself and me.

Jabberwocky

'Twas brillig, and the slithy toves
    Did gyre and gimble in the wabe;
All mimsy were the borogoves,
    And the mome raths outgrabe.[1]

---

[1] Readers experiencing difficulty with this stanza should turn to p.120 for Humpty Dumpty's detailed explanation. – *Ed*.

'Beware the Jabberwock, my son!
    The jaws that bite, the claws that catch!
Beware the Jubjub bird, and shun
    The frumious Bandersnatch!'

He took his vorpal sword in hand:
    Long time the manxome foe he sought –
So rested he by the Tumtum tree,
    And stood awhile in thought.

And as in uffish thought he stood,
    The Jabberwock, with eyes of flame,
Came whiffling through the tulgey wood,
    And burbled as it came!

One, two! One, two! And through and through
    The vorpal blade went snicker-snack!
He left it dead, and with its head
    He went galumphing back.

'And hast thou slain the Jabberwock?
    Come to my arms, my beamish boy!
O frabjous day! Callooh! Callay!'
    He chortled in his joy.

'Twas brillig, and the slithy toves
    Did gyre and gimble in the wabe;
All mimsy were the borogoves,
    And the mome raths outgrabe.

THE JABBERWOCK, WITH EYES OF FLAME

The Walrus and the Carpenter

The sun was shining on the sea,
   Shining with all his might:
He did his very best to make
   The billows smooth and bright –
And this was odd, because it was
   The middle of the night.

The moon was shining sulkily,
   Because she thought the sun
Had got no business to be there
   After the day was done –
'It's very rude of him,' she said,
   'To come and spoil the fun!'

The sea was wet as wet could be,
   The sands were dry as dry.
You could not see a cloud, because
   No cloud was in the sky:
No birds were flying overhead –
   There were no birds to fly.

The Walrus and the Carpenter
    Were walking close at hand;
They wept like anything to see
    Such quantities of sand:
'If this were only cleared away,'
    They said, 'it *would* be grand!'

'If seven maids with seven mops
    Swept it for half a year,
Do you suppose,' the Walrus said,
    'That they could get it clear?'
'I doubt it,' said the Carpenter,
    And shed a bitter tear.

'O Oysters, come and walk with us!'
    The Walrus did beseech.
'A pleasant walk, a pleasant talk,
    Along the briny beach:
We cannot do with more than four,
    To give a hand to each.'

The eldest Oyster looked at him,
    But never a word he said:
The eldest Oyster winked his eye,
    And shook his heavy head –
Meaning to say he did not choose
    To leave the oyster-bed.

But four young Oysters hurried up,
    All eager for the treat:
Their coats were brushed, their faces washed,
    Their shoes were clean and neat –
And this was odd, because, you know,
    They hadn't any feet.

Four other Oysters followed them,
    And yet another four;
And thick and fast they came at last,
    And more, and more, and more –
All hopping through the frothy waves,
    And scrambling to the shore.

The Walrus and the Carpenter
    Walked on a mile or so,
And then they rested on a rock
    Conveniently low:
And all the little Oysters stood
    And waited in a row.

'The time has come,' the Walrus said,
    'To talk of many things:
Of shoes – and ships – and sealing-wax –
    Of cabbages – and kings –
And why the sea is boiling hot –
    And whether pigs have wings.'

'But wait a bit,' the Oysters cried,
  'Before we have our chat;
For some of us are out of breath,
  And all of us are fat!'
'No hurry!' said the Carpenter.
  They thanked him much for that.

'A loaf of bread,' the Walrus said,
  'Is what we chiefly need:
Pepper and vinegar besides
  Are very good indeed –
Now if you're ready, Oysters dear,
  We can begin to feed.'

'But not on us!' the Oysters cried,
  Turning a little blue.
'After such kindness, that would be
  A dismal thing to do!'
'The night is fine,' the Walrus said.
  'Do you admire the view?

'It was so kind of you to come!
  And you are very nice!'
The Carpenter said nothing but
  'Cut us another slice:
I wish you were not quite so deaf –
  I've had to ask you twice!'

'It seems a shame,' the Walrus said,
  'To play them such a trick,
After we've brought them out so far,
  And made them trot so quick!'
The Carpenter said nothing but
  'The butter's spread too thick!'

'I weep for you,' the Walrus said:
  'I deeply sympathize.'
With sobs and tears he sorted out
  Those of the largest size,
Holding his pocket-handkerchief
  Before his streaming eyes.

'O Oysters,' said the Carpenter,
  'You've had a pleasant run!
Shall we be trotting home again?'
  But answer came there none –
And this was scarcely odd, because
  They'd eaten every one.

Humpty Dumpty's Recitation

In winter, when the fields are white,
I sing this song for your delight –

In spring, when woods are getting green,
I'll try and tell you what I mean.

In summer, when the days are long,
Perhaps you'll understand the song:

In autumn, when the leaves are brown,
Take pen and ink, and write it down.

I sent a message to the fish:
I told them 'This is what I wish.'

The little fishes of the sea,
They sent an answer back to me.

The little fishes' answer was
'We cannot do it, Sir, because –'

I sent to them again to say
'It will be better to obey.'

The fishes answered with a grin,
'Why, what a temper you are in!'

I told them once, I told them twice:
They would not listen to advice.

I took a kettle large and new,
Fit for the deed I had to do.

My heart went hop, my heart went thump;
I filled my kettle at the pump.

Then someone came to me and said
'The little fishes are in bed.'

I said to him, I said it plain,
'Then you must wake them up again.'

I said it very loud and clear;
I went and shouted in his ear.

But he was very stiff and proud;
He said 'You needn't shout so loud!'

And he was very proud and stiff;
He said 'I'd go and wake them, if –'

I took a corkscrew from the shelf:
I went to wake them up myself.

And when I found the door was locked,
I pulled and pushed and kicked and knocked.

And when I found the door was shut,
I tried to turn the handle, but –

The White Knight's Ballad

I'll tell thee everything I can;
   There's little to relate.
I saw an aged aged man,
   A-sitting on a gate.
'Who are you, aged man?' I said.
   'And how is it you live?'
And his answer trickled through my head
   Like water through a sieve.

He said 'I look for butterflies
    That sleep among the wheat:
I make them into mutton-pies,
    And sell them in the street.
I sell them unto men,' he said,
    'Who sail on stormy seas;
And that's the way I get my bread –
    A trifle if you please.'

But I was thinking of a plan
    To dye one's whiskers green,
And always use so large a fan
    That they could not be seen.
So, having no reply to give
    To what the old man said,
I cried 'Come, tell me how you live!'
    And thumped him on the head.

His accents mild took up the tale:
    He said 'I go my ways,
And when I find a mountain-rill,
    I set it in a blaze;
And thence they make a stuff they call
    Rowland's Macassar Oil –
Yet twopence-halfpenny is all
    They give me for my toil.'

But I was thinking of a way
    To feed oneself on batter,
And so go on from day to day
    Getting a little fatter.
I shook him well from side to side,
    Until his face was blue:
'Come, tell me how you live,' I cried
    'And what it is you do!'

He said 'I hunt for haddocks' eyes
    Among the heather bright,

And work them into waistcoat-buttons
   In the silent night.
And these I do not sell for gold
   Or coin of silvery shine,
But for a copper halfpenny,
   And that will purchase nine.

'I sometimes dig for buttered rolls,
   Or set limed twigs for crabs;
I sometimes search the grassy knolls
   For wheels of hansom-cabs.
And that's the way' (he gave a wink)
   'By which I get my wealth –
And very gladly will I drink
   Your Honour's noble health.'

I heard him then, for I had just
   Completed my design
To keep the Menai bridge from rust
   By boiling it in wine.
I thanked him much for telling me
   The way he got his wealth,
But chiefly for his wish that he
   Might drink my noble health.

And now, if e'er by chance I put
   My fingers into glue,
Or madly squeeze a right-hand foot
   Into a left-hand shoe,
Or if I drop upon my toe
   A very heavy weight,
I weep, for it reminds me so
Of that old man I used to know –
Whose look was mild, whose speech was slow,
Whose hair was whiter than the snow,
Whose face was very like a crow,
With eyes, like cinders, all aglow,
Who seemed distracted with his woe,

Who rocked his body to and fro,
And muttered mumblingly and low,
As if his mouth were full of dough,
Who snorted like a buffalo –
That summer evening long ago
    A-sitting on a gate.

(Acrostic)

A boat, beneath a sunny sky,
Lingering onward dreamily
In an evening of July –

Children three that nestle near,
Eager eye and willing ear,
Pleased a simple tale to hear –

Long has paled that sunny sky:
Echoes fade and memories die:
Autumn frosts have slain July.

Still she haunts me, phantomwise,
Alice moving under skies
Never seen by waking eyes.

Children yet, the tale to hear,
Eager eye and willing ear,
Lovingly shall nestle near.

In a Wonderland they lie,
Dreaming as the days go by,
Dreaming as the summers die:

Ever drifting down the stream –
Lingering in the golden gleam –
Life, what is it but a dream?

Phantasmagoria

The Trystyng

One winter night, at half-past nine,
    Cold, tired, and cross, and muddy,
I had come home, too late to dine,
And supper, with cigars and wine,
    Was waiting in the study.

There was a strangeness in the room,
    And Something white and wavy
Was standing near me in the gloom –
I took it for the carpet-broom
    Left by that careless slavey.

But presently the Thing began
    To shiver and to sneeze:
On which I said 'Come, come, my man!
That's a most inconsiderate plan.
    Less noise there, if you please!'

'I've caught a cold,' the Thing replies,
    'Out there upon the landing.'
I turned to look in some surprise,
And there, before my very eyes,
    A little Ghost was standing!

He trembled when he caught my eye,
    And got behind a chair.
'How came you here,' I said, 'and why?
I never saw a thing so shy.
    Come out! Don't shiver there!'

He said 'I'd gladly tell you how,
    And also tell you why;
But' (here he gave a little bow)

'You're in so bad a temper now,
      You'd think it all a lie.

'And as to being in a fright,
      Allow me to remark
That Ghosts have just as good a right,
In every way, to fear the light,
      As Men to fear the dark.'

'No plea,' said I, 'can well excuse
      Such cowardice in you:
For Ghosts can visit when they choose,
Whereas we Humans can't refuse
      To grant the interview.'

He said 'A flutter of alarm
      Is not unnatural, is it?
I really feared you meant some harm:
But, now I see that you are calm,
      Let me explain my visit.

'Houses are classed, I beg to state,
      According to the number
Of Ghosts that they accommodate:
(The Tenant merely counts as *weight*,
      With Coals and other lumber).

'This is a "one-ghost" house, and you,
      When you arrived last summer,
May have remarked a Spectre who
Was doing all that Ghosts can do
      To welcome the new-comer.

'In Villas this is always done –
      However cheaply rented:
For, though of course there's less of fun
When there is only room for one,
      Ghosts have to be contented.

41

'That Spectre left you on the Third –
        Since then you've not been haunted:
For, as he never sent us word,
'Twas quite by accident we heard
        That any one was wanted.

'A Spectre has first choice, by right,
        In filling up a vacancy;
Then Phantom, Goblin, Elf, and Sprite –
If all these fail them, they invite
        The nicest Ghoul that they can see.

'The Spectres said the place was low,
        And that you kept bad wine:
So, as a Phantom had to go,
And I was first, of course, you know,
        I couldn't well decline.'

'No doubt,' said I, 'they settled who
        Was fittest to be sent:
Yet still to choose a brat like you,
To haunt a man of forty-two,
        Was no great compliment!'

'I'm not so young, Sir,' he replied,
        'As you might think. The fact is,
In caverns by the water-side,
And other places that I've tried,
        I've had a lot of practice:

'But I have never taken yet
        A strict domestic part,
And in my flurry I forget
The Five Good Rules of Etiquette
        We have to know by heart.'

My sympathies were warming fast
        Towards the little fellow:

He was so utterly aghast
At having found a Man at last,
　　　And looked so scared and yellow.

'At least,' I said, 'I'm glad to find
　　　A Ghost is not a *dumb* thing!
But pray sit down: you'll feel inclined
(If, like myself, you have not dined)
　　　To take a snack of something:

'Though, certainly, you don't appear
　　　A thing to offer *food* to!
And then I shall be glad to hear –
If you will say them loud and clear –
　　　The Rules that you allude to.'

'Thanks! You shall hear them by and by.
　　　This *is* a piece of luck!'
'What may I offer you?' said I.
'Well, since you *are* so kind, I'll try
　　　A little bit of duck.

'*One* slice! And may I ask you for
　　　Another drop of gravy?'
I sat and looked at him in awe,
For certainly I never saw
　　　A thing so white and wavy.

And still he seemed to grow more white,
　　　More vapoury, and wavier –
Seen in the dim and flickering light,
As he proceeded to recite
　　　His 'Maxims of Behaviour'.

Hys Fyve Rules

'My First – but don't suppose,' he said,
    'I'm setting you a riddle –
Is – if your Victim be in bed,
Don't touch the curtains at his head,
    But take them in the middle,

'And wave them slowly in and out,
    While drawing them asunder;
And in a minute's time, no doubt,
He'll raise his head and look about
    With eyes of wrath and wonder.

'And here you must on no pretence
    Make the first observation.
Wait for the Victim to commence:
No Ghost of any common sense
    Begins a conversation.

'If he should say *"How came you here?"*
    (The way that *you* began, Sir,)
In such a case your course is clear –
"On the bat's back, my little dear!"
    Is the appropriate answer.

'If after this he says no more,
    You'd best perhaps curtail your
Exertions – go and shake the door,
And then, if he begins to snore,
    You'll know the thing's a failure.

'By day, if he should be alone –
    At home or on a walk –
You merely give a hollow groan,
To indicate the kind of tone
    In which you mean to talk.

'But if you find him with his friends,
      The thing is rather harder.
In such a case success depends
On picking up some candle-ends,
      Or butter, in the larder.

'With this you make a kind of slide
      (It answers best with suet),
On which you must contrive to glide,
And swing yourself from side to side –
      One soon learns how to do it.

'The Second tells us what is right
      In ceremonious calls: –
"First burn a blue or crimson light"
(A thing I quite forgot to-night),
      "Then scratch the door or walls." '

I said 'You'll visit *here* no more,
      If you attempt the Guy.
I'll have no bonfires on *my* floor –
And, as for scratching at the door,
      I'd like to see you try!'

'The Third was written to protect
      The interests of the Victim,
And tells us, as I recollect,
To treat him with a grave respect,
      And not to contradict him.'

'That's plain,' said I, 'as Tare and Tret,
      To any comprehension:
I only wish *some* Ghosts I've met
Would not so *constantly* forget
      The maxim that you mention!'

'Perhaps,' he said, '*you* first transgressed
      The laws of hospitality:

All Ghosts instinctively detest
The Man that fails to treat his guest
  With proper cordiality.

'If you address a Ghost as "Thing!"
  Or strike him with a hatchet,
He is permitted by the King
To drop all *formal* parleying –
  And then you're *sure* to catch it!

'The Fourth prohibits trespassing
  Where other Ghosts are quartered:
And those convicted of the thing
(Unless when pardoned by the King)
  Must instantly be slaughtered.

'That simply means "be cut up small":
  Ghosts soon unite anew:
The process scarcely hurts at all –
Not more than when *you*'re what you call
  "Cut up" by a Review.

"The Fifth is one you may prefer
  That I should quote entire: –
The King must be addressed as "Sir".
This, from a simple courtier,
  Is all the Laws require:

'*But, should you wish to do the thing*
  With out-and-out politeness,
Accost him as "My Goblin King!"
And always use, in answering,
  The phrase "Your Royal Whiteness!"

'I'm getting rather hoarse, I fear,
  After so much reciting:
So, if you don't object, my dear,
We'll try a glass of bitter beer –
  I think it looks inviting.'

46

CANTO III

Scarmoges

'And did you really walk,' said I,
　　'On such a wretched night?
I always fancied Ghosts could fly –
If not exactly in the sky,
　　Yet at a fairish height.'

'It's very well,' said he, 'for Kings
　　To soar above the earth:
But Phantoms often find that wings –
Like many other pleasant things –
　　Cost more than they are worth.

'Spectres of course are rich, and so
　　Can buy them from the Elves:
But *we* prefer to keep below –
They're stupid company, you know,
　　For any but themselves:

'For, though they claim to be exempt
　　From pride, they treat a Phantom
As something quite beneath contempt –
Just as no Turkey ever dreamt
　　Of noticing a Bantam.'

'They seem too proud,' said I, 'to go
　　To houses such as mine.
Pray, how did they contrive to know
So quickly that "the place was low,"
　　And that I "kept bad wine"?'

'Inspector Kobold came to you –'
　　The little Ghost began.
Here I broke in – 'Inspector who?
Inspecting Ghosts is something new!
　　Explain yourself, my man!'

'His name is Kobold,' said my guest:
        'One of the Spectre order:
You'll very often see him dressed
In a yellow gown, a crimson vest,
        And a night-cap with a border.

'He tried the Brocken business first,
        But caught a sort of chill;
So came to England to be nursed,
And here it took the form of *thirst*,
        Which he complains of still.

'Port-wine, he says, when rich and sound,
        Warms his old bones like nectar:
And as the inns, where it is found,
Are his especial hunting-ground,
        We call him the *Inn-Spectre*.'

I bore it – bore it like a man –
        This agonizing witticism!
And nothing could be sweeter than
My temper, till the Ghost began
        Some most provoking criticism.

'Cooks need not be indulged in waste;
        Yet still you'd better teach them
Dishes should have *some sort* of taste.
Pray, why are all the cruets placed
        Where nobody can reach them?

'That man of yours will never earn
        His living as a waiter!
Is that queer *thing* supposed to burn?
(It's far too dismal a concern
        To call a Moderator.)

'The duck was tender, but the peas
        Were very much too old:

And just remember, if you please,
The *next* time you have toasted cheese,
    Don't let them send it cold.

'You'd find the bread improved, I think,
    By getting better flour:
And have you anything to drink
That looks a *little* less like ink,
    And isn't *quite* so sour?'

Then, peering round with curious eyes,
    He muttered 'Goodness gracious!'
And so went on to criticize –
'Your room's an inconvenient size:
    It's neither snug nor spacious.

'That narrow window, I expect,
    Serves but to let the dusk in –'
'But please,' said I, 'to recollect
'Twas fashioned by an architect
    Who pinned his faith on Ruskin!'

'I don't care who he was, Sir, or
    On whom he pinned his faith!
Constructed by whatever law,
So poor a job I never saw,
    As I'm a living Wraith!

'What a re-markable cigar!
    How much are they a dozen?'
I growled 'No matter what they are!
You're getting as familiar
    As if you were my cousin!

'Now that's a thing *I will not stand*,
    And so I tell you flat.'
'Aha,' said he, 'we're getting grand!'
(Taking a bottle in his hand)
    'I'll soon arrange for *that*!'

And here he took a careful aim,
    And gaily cried 'Here goes!'
I tried to dodge it as it came,
But somehow caught it, all the same,
    Exactly on my nose.

And I remember nothing more
    That I can clearly fix,
Till I was sitting on the floor,
Repeating 'Two and five are four,
    But *five and two* are six.'

What really passed I never learned,
    Nor guessed: I only know
That, when at last my sense returned,
The lamp, neglected, dimly burned –
    The fire was getting low –

Through driving mists I seemed to see
    A Thing that smirked and smiled:
And found that he was giving me
A lesson in Biography,
    As if I were a child.

CANTO IV

Hys Nouryture

'Oh, when I was a little Ghost,
    A merry time had we!
Each seated on his favourite post,
We chumped and chawed the buttered toast
    They gave us for our tea.'

'That story is in print!' I cried.
    'Don't say it's not, because
It's known as well as Bradshaw's Guide!'
(The Ghost uneasily replied
    He hardly thought it was.)

'It's not in Nursery Rhymes? And yet
          I almost think it is –
"Three little Ghosteses" were set
"On posteses," you know, and ate
          Their "buttered toasteses".

'I have the book; so if you doubt it –'
          I turned to search the shelf.
'Don't stir!' he cried. 'We'll do without it:
I now remember all about it;
          I wrote the thing myself.

'It came out in a "Monthly", or
          At least my agent said it did:
Some literary swell, who saw
It, thought it seemed adapted for
          The Magazine he edited.

'My father was a Brownie, Sir;
          My mother was a fairy.
The notion had occurred to her,
The children would be happier,
          If they were taught to vary.

'The notion soon became a craze;
          And, when it once began, she
Brought us all out in different ways –
One was a Pixy, two were Fays,
          Another was a Banshee;

'The Fetch and Kelpie went to school
          And gave a lot of trouble;
Next came a Poltergeist and Ghoul,
And then two Trolls (which broke the rule),
          A Goblin, and a Double –

'(If that's a snuff-box on the shelf,'
          He added with a yawn,

'I'll take a pinch) – next came an Elf,
And then a Phantom (that's myself),
　　　And last, a Leprechaun.

'One day, some Spectres chanced to call,
　　　Dressed in the usual white:
I stood and watched them in the hall,
And couldn't make them out at all,
　　　They seemed so strange a sight.

'I wondered what on earth they were,
　　　That looked all head and sack;
But Mother told me not to stare,
And then she twitched me by the hair,
　　　And punched me in the back.

'Since then I've often wished that I
　　　Had been a Spectre born.
But what's the use?' (He heaved a sigh.)
'*They* are the ghost-nobility,
　　　And look on *us* with scorn.

'My phantom-life was soon begun:
　　　When I was barely six,
I went out with an older one –
And just at first I thought it fun,
　　　And learned a lot of tricks.

'I've haunted dungeons, castles, towers –
　　　Wherever I was sent:
I've often sat and howled for hours,
Drenched to the skin with driving showers,
　　　Upon a battlement.

'It's quite old-fashioned now to groan
　　　When you begin to speak:
This is the newest thing in tone –'
And here (it chilled me to the bone)
　　　He gave an *awful* squeak.

'Perhaps,' he added, 'to *your* ear
    That sounds an easy thing?
Try it yourself, my little dear!
It took *me* something like a year,
    With constant practising.

'And when you've learned to squeak, my man,
    And caught the double sob,
You're pretty much where you began:
Just try and gibber if you can!
    That's something *like* a job!

'*I've* tried it, and can only say
    I'm sure you couldn't do it, e-
ven if you practised night and day,
Unless you have a turn that way,
    And natural ingenuity.

'Shakespeare I think it is who treats
    Of Ghosts, in days of old,
Who "gibbered in the Roman streets",
Dressed, if you recollect, in sheets –
    They must have found it cold.

'I've often spent ten pounds on stuff,
    In dressing as a Double;
But, though it answers as a puff,
It never has effect enough
    To make it worth the trouble.

'Long bills soon quenched the little thirst
    I had for being funny.
The setting-up is always worst:
Such heaps of things you want at first,
    One must be made of money!

'For instance, take a Haunted Tower,
    With skull, cross-bones, and sheet;

Blue lights to burn (say) two an hour,
Condensing lens of extra power,
    And set of chains complete:

'What with the things you have to hire –
    The fitting on the robe –
And testing all the coloured fire –
The outfit of itself would tire
    The patience of a Job!

'And then they're so fastidious,
    The Haunted-House Committee:
I've often known them make a fuss
Because a Ghost was French, or Russ,
    Or even from the City!

'Some dialects are objected to –
    For one, the *Irish* brogue is:
And then, for all you have to do,
One pound a week they offer you,
    And find yourself in Bogies!'

CANTO V

Byckerment

'Don't they consult the "Victims", though?'
    I said. 'They should, by rights,
Give them a chance – because, you know,
The tastes of people differ so,
    Especially in Sprites.'

The Phantom shook his head and smiled.
    'Consult them? Not a bit!
'Twould be a job to drive one wild,
To satisfy one single child –
    There'd be no end to it!'

54

'Of course you can't leave *children* free,'
    Said I, 'to pick and choose:
But, in the case of men like me,
I think "Mine Host" might fairly be
    Allowed to state his views.'

He said 'It really wouldn't pay –
    Folk are so full of fancies.
We visit for a single day,
And whether then we go, or stay,
    Depends on circumstances.

'And, though we don't consult "Mine Host"
    Before the thing's arranged,
Still, if he often quits his post,
Or is not a well-mannered Ghost,
    Then you can have him changed.

'But if the host's a man like you –
    I mean a man of sense;
And if the house is not too new –'
'Why, what has *that*,' said I, 'to do
    With Ghost's convenience?'

'A new house does not suit, you know –
    It's such a job to trim it:
But, after twenty years or so,
The wainscotings begin to go,
    So twenty is the limit.'

'To trim' was not a phrase I could
    Remember having heard:
'Perhaps,' I said, 'you'll be so good
As tell me what is understood
    Exactly by that word?'

'It means the loosening all the doors,'
    The Ghost replied, and laughed:

55

'It means the drilling holes by scores
In all the skirting-boards and floors,
    To make a thorough draught.

'You'll sometimes find that one or two
    Are all you really need
To let the wind come whistling through –
But *here* there'll be a lot to do!'
    I faintly gasped 'Indeed!

'If I'd been rather later, I'll
    Be bound,' I added, trying
(Most unsuccessfully) to smile,
'You'd have been busy all this while,
    Trimming and beautifying?'

'Why, no,' said he; 'perhaps I should
    Have stayed another minute –
But still no Ghost, that's any good,
Without an introduction would
    Have ventured to begin it.

'The proper thing, as you were late,
    Was certainly to go:
But, with the roads in such a state,
I got the Knight-Mayor's leave to wait
    For half an hour or so.'

'Who's the Knight-Mayor?' I cried. Instead
    Of answering my question,
'Well, if you don't know *that*,' he said,
'Either you never go to bed,
    Or you've a grand digestion!

'He goes about and sits on folk
    That eat too much at night:
His duties are to pinch, and poke,
And squeeze them till they nearly choke.'
    (I said 'It serves them right!')

'And folk who sup on things like these –'
　　He muttered, 'eggs and bacon –
Lobster – and duck – and toasted cheese –
If they don't get an awful squeeze,
　　I'm very much mistaken!

'He is immensely fat, and so
　　Well suits the occupation:
In point of fact, if you must know,
We used to call him years ago,
　　The Mayor and Corporation!!

'The day he was elected Mayor
　　I *know* that every Sprite meant
To vote for *me*, but did not dare –
He was so frantic with despair
　　And furious with excitement.

'When it was over, for a whim,
　　He ran to tell the King;
And being the reverse of slim,
A two-mile trot was not for him
　　A very easy thing.

'So, to reward him for his run
　　(As it was baking hot,
And he was over twenty stone),
The King proceeded, half in fun,
　　To knight him on the spot.'

'"Twas a great liberty to take!'
　　(I fired up like a rocket.)
'He did it just for punning's sake:
"The man," says Johnson, "that would make
　　A pun, would pick a pocket!"'

'A man,' said he, 'is not a King.'
　　I argued for a while,

And did my best to prove the thing –
The Phantom merely listening
      With a contemptuous smile.

At last, when, breath and patience spent,
      I had recourse to smoking –
'Your *aim*,' he said, 'is excellent:
But – when you call it *argument* –
      Of course you're only joking?'

Stung by his cold and snaky eye,
      I roused myself at length
To say, 'At least I do defy
The veriest sceptic to deny
      That union is strength!'

'That's true enough,' said he, 'yet stay –'
      I listened in all meekness –
'*Union* is strength, I'm bound to say;
In fact, the thing's as clear as day;
      But *onions* are a weakness.'

CANTO VI

Dyscomfyture

As one who strives a hill to climb,
      Who never climbed before:
Who finds it, in a little time,
Grow every moment less sublime,
      And votes the thing a bore:

Yet, having once begun to try,
      Dares not desert his quest,
But, climbing, ever keeps his eye
On one small hut against the sky
      Wherein he hopes to rest:

58

Who climbs till nerve and force are spent,
    With many a puff and pant:
Who still, as rises the ascent,
In language grows more violent,
    Although in breath more scant:

Who, climbing, gains at length the place
    That crowns the upward track:
And, entering with unsteady pace,
Receives a buffet in the face
    That lands him on his back:

And feels himself, like one in sleep,
    Glide swiftly down again,
A helpless weight, from steep to steep,
Till, with a headlong giddy sweep,
    He drops upon the plain –

So I, that had resolved to bring
    Conviction to a ghost,
And found it quite a different thing
From any human arguing,
    Yet dared not quit my post.

But, keeping still the end in view
    To which I hoped to come,
I strove to prove the matter true
By putting everything I knew
    Into an axiom:

Commencing every single phrase
    With 'therefore' or 'because',
I blindly reeled, a hundred ways,
About the syllogistic maze,
    Unconscious where I was.

Quoth he 'That's regular clap-trap:
    Don't bluster any more.

Now *do* be cool and take a nap!
Such a ridiculous old chap
  Was never seen before!

'You're like a man I used to meet,
  Who got one day so furious
In arguing, the simple heat
Scorched both his slippers off his feet!'
  I said *'That's very curious!'*

'Well, it *is* curious, I agree,
  And sounds perhaps like fibs:
But still it's true as true can be –
As sure as your name's Tibbs,' said he.
  I said 'My name's *not* Tibbs.'

'*Not* Tibbs!' he cried – his tone became
  A shade or two less hearty –
'Why, no,' said I. 'My proper name
Is Tibbets –' 'Tibbets?' 'Aye, the same.'
  'Why, then YOU'RE NOT THE PARTY!'

With that he struck the board a blow
  That shivered half the glasses.
'Why couldn't you have told me so
Three quarters of an hour ago,
  You prince of all the asses?

'To walk four miles through mud and rain,
  To spend the night in smoking,
And then to find that it's in vain –
And I've to do it all again –
  It's really *too* provoking!

'Don't talk!' he cried, as I began
  To mutter some excuse.
'Who can have patience with a man
That's got no more discretion than
  An idiotic goose?

'To keep me waiting here, instead
      Of telling me at once
That this was not the house!' he said.
'There, that'll do – be off to bed!
      Don't gape like that, you dunce!'

'It's very fine to throw the blame
      On *me* in such a fashion!
Why didn't you enquire my name
The very minute that you came?'
      I answered in a passion.

'Of course it worries you a bit
      To come so far on foot –
But how was *I* to blame for it?'
'Well, well!' said he. 'I must admit
      That isn't badly put.

'And certainly you've given me
      The best of wine and victual –
Excuse my violence,' said he,
'But accidents like this, you see,
      They put one out a little.

''Twas *my* fault after all, I find –
      Shake hands, old Turnip-top!'
The name was hardly to my mind,
But, as no doubt he meant it kind,
      I let the matter drop.

'Goodnight, old Turnip-top, good-night!
      When I am gone, perhaps
They'll send you some inferior Sprite,
Who'll keep you in a constant fright
      And spoil your soundest naps.

'Tell him you'll stand no sort of trick;
      Then, if he leers and chuckles,
You just be handy with a stick

(Mind that it's pretty hard and thick)
    And rap him on the knuckles!

'Then carelessly remark "Old coon!
    Perhaps you're not aware
That, if you don't behave, you'll soon
Be chuckling to another tune –
    And so you'd best take care!"

'That's the right way to cure a Sprite
    Of such-like goings-on –
But gracious me! It's getting light!
Good-night, old Turnip-top, good-night!'
    A nod, and he was gone.

CANTO VII

Sad Souvenaunce

'What's this?' I pondered. 'Have I slept?'
    Or can I have been drinking?'
But soon a gentler feeling crept
Upon me, and I sat and wept
    An hour or so, like winking.

'No need for Bones to hurry so!'
    I sobbed. 'In fact, I doubt
If it was worth his while to go –
And who is Tibbs, I'd like to know,
    To make such work about?

'If Tibbs is anything like me,
    It's *possible*,' I said
'He won't be over-pleased to be
Dropped in upon at half-past three,
    After he's snug in bed.

'And if Bones plagues him anyhow –
    Squeaking and all the rest of it,

As he was doing here just now –
I prophesy there'll be a row,
    And Tibbs will have the best of it!'

Then, as my tears could never bring
    The friendly Phantom back,
It seemed to me the proper thing
To mix another glass, and sing
    The following Coronach.

And art thou gone, beloved Ghost?
    Best of Familiars!
Nay then, farewell, my duckling roast,
Farewell, farewell, my tea and toast,
    My meerschaum and cigars!

The hues of life are dull and gray,
    The sweets of life insipid,
When thou, *my charmer, art away –*
Old Brick, or rather, let me say,
    Old Parallelepiped!

Instead of singing Verse the Third,
    I ceased – abruptly, rather:
But, after such a splendid word
I felt that it would be absurd
    To try it any farther.

So with a yawn I went my way
    To seek the welcome downy,
And slept, and dreamed till break of day
Of Poltergeist and Fetch and Fay
    And Leprechaun and Brownie!

For years I've not been visited
    By any kind of Sprite;
Yet still they echo in my head,
Those parting words, so kindly said,
    'Old Turnip-top, good-night!'

A Sea Dirge

There are certain things – as, a spider, a ghost,
   The income-tax, gout, an umbrella for three –
That I hate, but the thing I hate the most
    Is a thing they call the Sea.

Pour some salt water over the floor –
   Ugly I'm sure you'll allow it to be:
Suppose it extended a mile or more,
    That's very like the Sea.

Beat a dog till it howls outright –
   Cruel, but all very well for a spree:
Suppose that he did so day and night,
    That would be like the Sea.

I had a vision of nursery-maids;
   Tens of thousands passed by me –
All leading children with wooden spades,
    And this was by the Sea.

Who invented those spades of wood?
   Who was it cut them out of the tree?
None, I think, but an idiot could –
    Or one that loved the Sea.

It is pleasant and dreamy, no doubt, to float
   With 'thoughts as boundless, and souls as free':
But, suppose you are very unwell in the boat,
    How do you like the Sea?

There is an insect that people avoid
   (Whence is derived the verb 'to flee').
Where have you been by it most annoyed?
    In lodgings by the Sea.

If you like your coffee with sand for dregs,
    A decided hint of salt in your tea,
And a fishy taste in the very eggs –
        By all means choose the Sea.

And if, with these dainties to drink and eat,
    You prefer not a vestige of grass or tree,
And a chronic state of wet in your feet,
        Then – I recommend the Sea.

For *I* have friends who dwell by the coast –
    Pleasant friends they are to me!
It is when I am with them I wonder most
        That anyone likes the Sea.

They take me a walk: though tired and stiff,
    To climb the heights I madly agree;
And, after a tumble or so from the cliff,
        They kindly suggest the Sea.

I try the rocks, and I think it cool
    That they laugh with such an excess of glee,
As I heavily slip into every pool
        That skirts the cold cold Sea.

Hiawatha's Photographing

[In an age of imitation, I can claim no special merit for this slight attempt at doing what is known to be so easy. Any fairly practised writer, with the slightest ear for rhythm, could compose, for hours together, in the easy running metre of 'The Song of Hiawatha'. Having, then, distinctly stated that I challenge no attention in the following little poem to its merely verbal jingle, I must beg the candid reader to confine his criticism to its treatment of the subject.[1]]

From his shoulder Hiawatha
Took the camera of rosewood,
Made of sliding, folding rosewood;
Neatly put it all together
In its case it lay compactly,
Folded into nearly nothing;
But he opened out the hinges,
Pushed and pulled the joints and hinges,
Till it looked all squares and oblongs,
Like a complicated figure
In the Second Book of Euclid.

This he perched upon a tripod –
Crouched beneath its dusky cover –
Stretched his hand, enforcing silence –
Said, 'Be motionless, I beg you!'
Mystic, awful was the process.

All the family sat in order
Sat before him for their pictures:
Each in turn, as he was taken,
Volunteered his own suggestions,
His ingenious suggestions.

First the Governor, the Father:
He suggested velvet curtains

---

[1] The introductory paragraph also follows 'the easy running metre of "The Song of Hiawatha".' – *Ed*.

Looped about a massy pillar;
And the corner of a table,
Of a rosewood dining-table.
He would hold a scroll of something,
Hold it firmly in his left-hand;
He would keep his right-hand buried
(Like Napoleon) in his waistcoat;
He would contemplate the distance
With a look of pensive meaning,
As of ducks that die in tempests.

Grand, heroic was the notion:
Yet the picture failed entirely:
Failed, because he moved a little,
Moved, because he couldn't help it.

Next, his better half took courage;
She would have her picture taken.
She came dressed beyond description,
Dressed in jewels and in satin
Far too gorgeous for an empress.
Gracefully she sat down sideways,
With a simper scarcely human,
Holding in her hand a bouquet
Rather larger than a cabbage.
All the while that she was sitting,
Still the lady chattered, chattered,
Like a monkey in the forest.
'Am I sitting still?' she asked him.
'Is my face enough in profile?
Shall I hold the bouquet higher?
Will it come into the picture?'
And the picture failed completely.

Next the Son, the Stunning-Cantab:
He suggested curves of beauty,
Curves pervading all his figure,
Which the eye might follow onward,
Till they centred in the breast-pin,
Centred in the golden breast-pin.
He had learnt it all from Ruskin

(Author of *The Stones of Venice*,
Seven Lamps of Architecture,
Modern Painters, and some others);
And perhaps he had not fully
Understood his author's meaning;
But, whatever was the reason,
All was fruitless, as the picture
Ended in an utter failure.

Next to him the eldest daughter:
She suggested very little,
Only asked if he would take her
With her look of 'passive beauty'.

Her idea of passive beauty
Was a squinting of the left-eye,
Was a drooping of the right-eye,
Was a smile that went up sideways
To a corner of the nostrils.

Hiawatha, when she asked him,
Took no notice of the question,
Looked as if he hadn't heard it;
But, when pointedly appealed to,
Smiled in his peculiar manner,
Coughed and said it 'didn't matter',
Bit his lip and changed the subject.

Nor in this was he mistaken,
As the picture failed completely.

So in turn the other sisters.

Last, the youngest son was taken:
Very rough and thick his hair was,
Very round and red his face was,
Very dusty was his jacket,
Very fidgety his manner.
And his overbearing sisters
Called him names he disapproved of:
Called him Johnny, 'Daddy's Darling',
Called him Jacky, 'Scrubby School-boy'.
And, so awful was the picture,
In comparison the others

Seemed, to one's bewildered fancy,
To have partially succeeded.
    Finally my Hiawatha
Tumbled all the tribe together,
('Grouped' is not the right expression),
And, as happy chance would have it
Did at last obtain a picture
Where the faces all succeeded:
Each came out a perfect likeness.
    Then they joined and all abused it,
Unrestrainedly abused it,
As the worst and ugliest picture
They could possibly have dreamed of.
'Giving one such strange expressions –
Sullen, stupid, pert expressions.
Really any one would take us
(Any one that did not know us)
For the most unpleasant people!'
(Hiawatha seemed to think so,
Seemed to think it not unlikely).
All together rang their voices,
Angry, loud, discordant voices,
As of dogs that howl in concert,
As of cats that wail in chorus.
    But my Hiawatha's patience,
His politeness and his patience,
Unaccountably had vanished,
And he left that happy party.
Neither did he leave them slowly,
With the calm deliberation,
The intense deliberation
Of a photographic artist:
But he left them in a hurry,
Left them in a mighty hurry,
Stating that he would not stand it,
Stating in emphatic language
What he'd be before he'd stand it.
Hurriedly he packed his boxes:

Hurriedly the porter trundled
On a barrow all his boxes:
Hurriedly he took his ticket:
Hurriedly the train received him:
Thus departed Hiawatha.

Poeta Fit, Non Nascitur

'How shall I be a poet?
　　How shall I write in rhyme:
You told me once "the very wish
　　Partook of the sublime."
Then tell me how! Don't put me off
　　With your "another time"!'

The old man smiled to see him,
　　To hear his sudden sally;
He liked the lad to speak his mind
　　Enthusiastically;
And thought 'There's no hum-drum in him,
　　Nor any shilly-shally.'

'And would you be a poet
　　Before you've been to school?
Ah, well! I hardly thought you
　　So absolute a fool.
First learn to be spasmodic –
　　A very simple rule.

'For first you write a sentence,
　　And then you chop it small;
Then mix the bits, and sort them out
　　Just as they chance to fall:
The order of the phrases makes
　　No difference at all.

'Then, if you'd be impressive,
    Remember what I say,
That abstract qualities begin
    With capitals alway:
The True, the Good, the Beautiful –
    Those are the things that pay!

'Next, when you are describing
    A shape, or sound, or tint;
Don't state the matter plainly,
    But put it in a hint;
And learn to look at all things
    With a sort of mental squint.'

'For instance, if I wished, Sir,
    Of mutton-pies to tell,
Should I say "dreams of fleecy flocks
    Pent in a wheaten cell"?'
'Why, yes,' the old man said: 'that phrase
    Would answer very well.

'Then fourthly, there are epithets
    That suit with any word –
As well as Harvey's Reading Sauce
    With fish, or flesh, or bird –
Of these, "wild", "lonely", "weary", "strange",
    Are much to be preferred.'

'And will it do, O will it do
    To take them in a lump –
As "the wild man went his weary way
    To a strange and lonely pump"?'
'Nay, nay! You must not hastily
    To such conclusions jump.

'Such epithets, like pepper
    Give zest to what you write;
And, if you strew them sparely,

71

They whet the appetite:
But if you lay them on too thick,
   You spoil the matter quite!

'Last, as to the arrangement:
   Your reader, you should show him,
Must take what information he
   Can get, and look for no im-
mature disclosure of the drift
   And purpose of your poem.

'Therefore, to test his patience –
   How much he can endure –
Mention no places, names, or dates,
   And evermore be sure
Throughout the poem to be found
   Consistently obscure.

'First fix upon the limit
   To which it shall extend:
Then fill it up with "Padding"
   (Beg some of any friend):
Your great SENSATION-STANZA
   You place towards the end.'

'And what is a Sensation,
   Grandfather, tell me, pray?
I think I never heard the word
   So used before to-day:
Be kind enough to mention one
   "*Exempli gratiâ.*"'

And the old man, looking sadly
   Across the garden-lawn,
Where here and there a dew-drop
   Yet glittered in the dawn,
Said 'Go to the Adelphi,
   And see the "Colleen Bawn".

'The word is due to Boucicault –
    The theory is his,
Where Life becomes a Spasm,
    And History a Whiz:
If that is not Sensation,
    I don't know what it is.

'Now try your hand, ere Fancy
    Have lost its present glow –'
'And then,' his grandson added,
    'We'll publish it, you know:
Green cloth – gold-lettered at the back –
    In duodecimo!'

Then proudly smiled that old man
    To see the eager lad
Rush madly for his pen and ink
    And for his blotting-pad –
But, when he thought of *publishing*,
    His face grew stern and sad.

The Lang Coortin'

The ladye she stood at her lattice high,
    Wi' her doggie at her feet;
Thorough the lattice she can spy
    The passers in the street,

'There's one that standeth at the door,
    And tirleth at the pin:
Now speak and say, my popinjay,
    If I sall let him in.'

73

Then up and spake the popinjay
   That flew abune her head:
'Gae let him in that tirls the pin:
   He cometh thee to wed.'

O when he cam' the parlour in,
   A woeful man was he!
'And dinna ye ken your lover agen,
   Sae well that loveth thee?'

'And how wad I ken ye loved me, Sir,
   That have been sae lang away?
And how wad I ken ye loved me, Sir?
   Ye never telled me sae.'

Said – 'Ladye dear,' and the salt, salt tear
   Cam' rinnin' doon his cheek,
'I have sent the tokens of my love
   This many and many a week.

'O didna ye get the rings, Ladye,
   The rings o' the gowd sae fine?
I wot that I have sent to thee
   Four score, four score and nine.'

'They cam' to me,' said that fair ladye.
   'Wow, they were flimsie things!'
Said – 'that chain o' gowd, my doggie to howd,
   It is made o' thae self-same rings.'

'And didna ye get the locks, the locks,
   The locks o' my ain black hair,
Whilk I sent by post, whilk I sent by box,
   Whilk I sent by the carrier?'

'They cam' to me,' said that fair ladye;
   'And I prithee send nae mair!'
Said – 'that cushion sae red, for my doggie's head,
   It is stuffed wi' thae locks o' hair.'

'And didna ye get the letter, Ladye,
    Tied wi' a silken string,
Whilk I sent to thee frae the far countrie,
    A message of love to bring?'

'It cam' to me frae the far countrie
    Wi' its silken string and a';
But it wasna prepaid,' said that high-born maid,
    'Sae I gar'd them tak' it awa'.'

'O ever alack that ye sent it back,
    It was written sae clerkly and well!
Now the message it brought, and the boon that it sought,
    I must even say it mysel'.'

Then up and spake the popinjay,
    Sae wisely counselled he.
'Now say it in the proper way:
    Gae doon upon thy knee!'

The lover he turned baith red and pale,
    Went doon upon his knee:
'O Ladye, hear the waesome tale
    That must be told to thee!

'For five lang years, and five lang years,
    I coorted thee by looks;
By nods and winks, by smiles and tears,
    As I had read in books.

'For ten lang years, O weary hours!
    I coorted thee by signs;
By sending game, by sending flowers,
    By sending Valentines.

'For five lang years, and five lang years,
    I have dwelt in the far countrie,
Till that thy mind should be inclined
    Mair tenderly to me.

'Now thirty years are gane and past,
    I am come frae a foreign land:
I am come to tell thee my love at last –
    O Ladye, gie me thy hand!'

The ladye she turned not pale nor red,
    But she smiled a pitiful smile:
'Sic' a coortin' as yours, my man,' she said,
    'Takes a lang and a weary while!'

And out and laughed the popinjay,
    A laugh of bitter scorn:
'A coortin' done in sic' a way,
    It ought not to be borne!'

Wi' that the doggie barked aloud,
    And up and doon he ran,
And tugged and strained his chain o' gowd,
    All for to bite the man.

'O hush thee, gentle popinjay!
    O hush thee, doggie dear!
There is a word I fain wad say,
    It needeth he should hear!'

Aye louder screamed that ladye fair
    To drown her doggie's bark:
Ever the lover shouted mair
    To make that ladye hark:

Shrill and more shrill the popinjay
    Upraised his angry squall:
I trow that doggie's voice that day
    Was louder than them all!

The serving-men and serving-maids
    Sat by the kitchen fire:
They heard sic' a din the parlour within
    As made them much admire.

Out spake the boy in buttons
  (I ween he wasna thin),
'Now wha will tae the parlour gae,
  And stay this deadlie din?'

And they have taen a kerchief,
  Casted their kevils in,
For wha will tae the parlour gae,
  And stay that deadlie din.

When on that boy the kevil fell
  To stay the fearsome noise,
'Gae in,' they cried, 'whate'er betide,
  Thou prince of button-boys!'

Syne, he has taen a supple cane
  To swinge that dog sae fat:
The doggie yowled, the doggie howled
  The louder aye for that.

Syne, he has taen a mutton-bane –
  The doggie ceased his noise,
And followed doon the kitchen stair
  That prince of button-boys!

Then sadly spake that ladye fair,
  Wi' a frown upon her brow:
'O dearer to me is my sma' doggie
  Than a dozen sic' as thou!

'Nae use, nae use for sighs and tears:
  Nae use at all to fret:
Sin' ye've bided sae well for thirty years,
  Ye may bide a wee langer yet!'

Sadly, sadly he crossed the floor
  And tirlëd at the pin:
Sadly went he through the door
  Where sadly he cam' in.

'O gin I had a popinjay
  To fly abune my head,
To tell me what I ought to say,
  I had by this been wed.

'O gin I find anither ladye,'
  He said wi' sighs and tears,
'I wot my coortin' sall not be
  Anither thirty years.

'For gin I find a ladye gay,
  Exactly to my taste,
I'll pop the question, aye or nay,
  In twenty years at maist.'

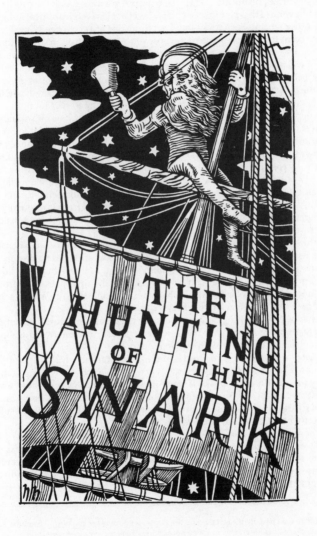

Preface

If – and the thing is wildly possible – the charge of writing nonsense were ever brought against the author of this brief but instructive poem, it would be based, I feel convinced, on the line, 'Then the bowsprit got mixed with the rudder sometimes.' In view of this painful possibility, I will not (as I might) appeal indignantly to my other writings as a proof that I am incapable of such a deed: I will not (as I might) point to the strong moral purpose of this poem itself, to the arithmetical principles so cautiously inculcated in it, or to its noble teachings in Natural History – I will take the more prosaic course of simply explaining how it happened.

The Bellman, who was almost morbidly sensitive about appearances, used to have the bowsprit unshipped once or twice a week to be revarnished, and it more than once happened, when the time came for replacing it, that no one on board could remember which end of the ship it belonged to. They knew it was not of the slightest use to appeal to the Bellman about it – he would only refer to his Naval Code, and read out in pathetic tones Admiralty Instructions which none of them had ever been able to understand – so it generally ended in its being fastened on anyhow, across the rudder. The helmsman[1] used to stand by with tears in his eyes: *he* knew it was all wrong, but alas! Rule 42 of the Code, '*No one shall speak to the Man at the Helm*', had been completed by the Bellman himself with the words '*and the Man at the Helm shall speak to no one.*' So remonstrance was impossible, and no steering could be done till the next varnishing day. During these bewildering intervals the ship usually sailed backwards.

As this poem is to some extent connected with the lay of the Jabberwock, let me take this opportunity of answering a question that has often been asked me, how to pronounce 'slithy toves'. The 'i' in 'slithy' is long, as in 'writhe'; and 'toves' is pronounced so as to rhyme with 'groves'. Again, the first 'o' in 'borogroves' is pronounced like the 'o' in 'borrow'. I have heard people try to give it the sound of the 'o' in 'worry'. Such is Human Perversity.

This also seems a fitting occasion to notice the other hard words in that poem. Humpty-Dumpty's theory, of two meanings packed into one word like a portmanteau, seems to me the right explanation for all.

For instance, take the two words 'fuming' and 'furious'. Make up your mind that you will say both words, but leave it unsettled which you will say first. Now open your mouth and speak. If your thoughts incline ever so little towards 'fuming', you will say 'fuming-furious'; if they turn, by even a hair's breadth, towards 'furious', you will say 'furious-fuming'; but if you have that rarest of gifts, a perfectly balanced mind, you will say 'frumious'.

Supposing that, when Pistol uttered the well-known words – 'Under which king, Bezonian? Speak or die!' Justice Shallow had felt certain that it was either William or Richard, but had not been able to settle which, so that he could not possibly say either name before the other, can it be doubted that, rather than die, he would have gasped out 'Rilchiam!'

---

[1] This office was usually undertaken by the Boots, who found in it a refuge from the Baker's constant complaints about the insufficient blacking of his three pair of boots.

Inscribed to a dear Child:
in memory of golden summer hours
and whispers of a summer sea

(ACROSTIC)

Girt with a boyish garb for boyish task,
    Eager she wields her spade: yet loves as well
Rest on a friendly knee, intent to ask
    The tale he loves to tell.

Rude spirits of the seething outer strife,
    Unmeet to read her pure and simple spright,
Deem, if you list, such hours a waste of life
    Empty of all delight!

Chat on, sweet Maid, and rescue from annoy
    Hearts that by wiser talk are unbeguiled.
Ah, happy he who owns that tenderest joy,
    The heart-love of a child!

Away, fond thoughts, and vex my soul no more!
    Work claims my wakeful nights, my busy days –
Albeit bright memories of that sunlit shore
    Yet haunt my dreaming gaze!

The Hunting of the Snark

An Agony, in Eight Fits

Fit the First

THE LANDING

'Just the place for a Snark!' the Bellman cried,
    As he landed his crew with care;
Supporting each man on the top of the tide
    By a finger entwined in his hair.

81

SUPPORTING EACH MAN ON THE TOP OF THE TIDE

'Just the place for a Snark! I have said it twice:
  That alone should encourage the crew.
Just the place for a Snark! I have said it thrice:
  What I tell you three times is true.'

The crew was complete: it included a Boots –
  A maker of Bonnets and Hoods –
A Barrister, brought to arrange their disputes –
  And a Broker, to value their goods.

A Billiard-marker, whose skill was immense,
  Might perhaps have won more than his share –
But a Banker, engaged at enormous expense,
  Had the whole of their cash in his care.

There was also a Beaver, that paced on the deck,
  Or would sit making lace in the bow:
And had often (the Bellman said) saved them from wreck,
  Though none of the sailors knew how.

There was one who was famed for the number of things
  He forgot when he entered the ship:
His umbrella, his watch, all his jewels and rings,
  And the clothes he had bought for the trip.

He had forty-two boxes, all carefully packed,
  With his name painted clearly on each:
But, since he omitted to mention the fact,
  They were all left behind on the beach.

The loss of his clothes hardly mattered, because
  He had seven coats on when he came,
With three pairs of boots – but the worst of it was,
  He had wholly forgotten his name.

He would answer to 'Hi!' or to any loud cry
  Such as 'Fry me!' or 'Fritter my wig!'
To 'What-you-may-call-um!' or 'What-was-his-name!'
  But especially 'Thing-um-a-jig!'

HE HAD WHOLLY FORGOTTEN HIS NAME

While, for those who preferred a more forcible word,
    He had different names from these:
His intimate friends called him 'Candle-ends',
    And his enemies 'Toasted-cheese'.

'His form is ungainly – his intellect small –'
    (So the Bellman would often remark)
'But his courage is perfect! And that, after all,
    Is the thing that one needs with a Snark.'

He would joke with hyænas, returning their stare
    With an impudent wag of the head:
And he once went a walk, paw-in-paw, with a bear,
    'Just to keep up its spirits,' he said.

He came as a Baker: but owned when too late –
    And it drove the poor Bellman half-mad –
He could only make Bridecake – for which, I may state,
    No materials were to be had.

The last of the crew needs especial remark,
    Though he looked an incredible dunce:
He had just one idea – but, that one being 'Snark',
    The good Bellman engaged him at once.

He came as a Butcher: but gravely declared,
    When the ship had been sailing a week,
He could only kill Beavers. The Bellman looked scared,
    And was almost too frightened to speak:

But at length he explained, in a tremulous tone,
    There was only one Beaver on board;
And that was a tame one he had of his own,
    Whose death would be deeply deplored.

The Beaver, who happened to hear the remark,
    Protested, with tears in its eyes,
That not even the rapture of hunting the Snark
    Could atone for that dismal surprise!

THE BEAVER KEPT LOOKING THE OPPOSITE WAY

It strongly advised that the Butcher should be
Conveyed in a separate ship:
But the Bellman declared that would never agree
With the plans he had made for the trip:

Navigation was always a difficult art,
Though with only one ship and one bell;
And he feared he must really decline, for his part,
Undertaking another as well.

The Beaver's best course was, no doubt, to procure
A second-hand dagger-proof coat –
So the Baker advised it – and next, to insure
Its life in some Office of note:

This the Banker suggested, and offered for hire
(On moderate terms), or for sale,
Two excellent Policies, one Against Fire,
And one Against Damage From Hail.

Yet still, ever after that sorrowful day,
Whenever the Butcher was by,
The Beaver kept looking the opposite way,
And appeared unaccountably shy.

Fit the Second

THE BELLMAN'S SPEECH

The Bellman himself they all praised to the skies –
Such a carriage, such ease and such grace!
Such solemnity, too! One could see he was wise,
The moment one looked in his face!

He had bought a large map representing the sea,
Without the least vestige of land:
And the crew were much pleased when they found it to be
A map they could all understand.

'What's the good of Mercator's North Poles and Equators,
  Tropics, Zones, and Meridian Lines?'
So the Bellman would cry: and the crew would reply,
  'They are merely conventional signs!

'Other maps are such shapes, with their islands and capes!
  But we've got our brave Captain to thank'
(So the crew would protest) 'that he's bought us the best –
  A perfect and absolute blank!'

This was charming, no doubt: but they shortly found out
  That the Captain they trusted so well
Had only one notion for crossing the ocean,
  And that was to tingle his bell.

He was thoughtful and grave – but the orders he gave
  Were enough to bewilder a crew.
When he cried, 'Steer to starboard, but keep her head larboard!'
  What on earth was the helmsman to do?

Then the bowsprit got mixed with the rudder sometimes:
  A thing, as the Bellman remarked,
That frequently happens in tropical climes,
  When a vessel is, so to speak, 'snarked'.

But the principal failing occurred in the sailing,
  And the Bellman, perplexed and distressed,
Said he *had* hoped, at least, when the wind blew due East
  That the ship would *not* travel due West!

But the danger was past – they had landed at last,
  With their boxes, portmanteaus, and bags:
Yet at first sight the crew were not pleased with the view,
  Which consisted of chasms and crags.

The Bellman perceived that their spirits were low,
  And repeated in musical tone
Some jokes he had kept for a season of woe –
  But the crew would do nothing but groan.

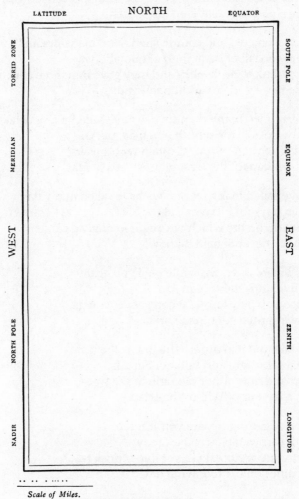

Scale of Miles.

OCEAN-CHART.

He served out some grog with a liberal hand,
  And bade them sit down on the beach:
And they could not but own that their Captain looked grand,
  As he stood and delivered his speech.

'Friends, Romans, and countrymen, lend me your ears!'
  (They were all of them fond of quotations:
So they drank to his health, and they gave him three cheers,
  While he served out additional rations.)

'We have sailed many months, we have sailed many weeks
  (Four weeks to the month you may mark),
But never as yet ('tis your Captain who speaks)
  Have we caught the least glimpse of a Snark!

'We have sailed many weeks, we have sailed many days
  (Seven days to the week I allow),
But a Snark, on the which we might lovingly gaze,
  We have never beheld till now!

'Come, listen, my men, while I tell you again
  The five unmistakable marks
By which you may know, wheresoever you go,
  The warranted genuine Snarks.

'Let us take them in order. The first is the taste,
  Which is meagre and hollow, but crisp:
Like a coat that is rather too tight in the waist,
  With a flavour of Will-o'-the-wisp.

'Its habit of getting up late you'll agree
  That it carries too far, when I say
That it frequently breakfasts at five-o'clock tea,
  And dines on the following day.

'The third is its slowness in taking a jest,
  Should you happen to venture on one,
It will sigh like a thing that is deeply distressed:
  And it always looks grave at a pun.

'The fourth is its fondness for bathing-machines,
   Which it constantly carries about,
And believes that they add to the beauty of scenes –
   A sentiment open to doubt.

'The fifth is ambition. It next will be right
   To describe each particular batch:
Distinguishing those that have feathers, and bite,
   From those that have whiskers, and scratch.

'For, although common Snarks do no manner of harm,
   Yet, I feel it my duty to say,
Some are Boojums –' The Bellman broke off in alarm,
   For the Baker had fainted away.

Fit the Third

THE BAKER'S TALE

They roused him with muffins – they roused him with ice –
   They roused him with mustard and cress –
They roused him with jam and judicious advice –
   They set him conundrums to guess.

When at length he sat up and was able to speak,
   His sad story he offered to tell;
And the Bellman cried 'Silence! not even a shriek!'
   And excitedly tingled his bell.

There was silence supreme! Not a shriek, not a scream,
   Scarcely even a howl or a groan,
As the man they called 'Ho!' told his story of woe
   In an antediluvian tone.

'My father and mother were honest, though poor –'
   'Skip all that!' cried the Bellman in haste.
'If it once becomes dark, there's no chance of a Snark –
   We have hardly a minute to waste!'

"BUT OH, BEAMISH NEPHEW, BEWARE OF THE DAY"

'I skip forty years,' said the Baker, in tears,
  'And proceed without further remark
To the day when you took me aboard of your ship
  To help you in hunting the Snark.

'A dear uncle of mine (after whom I was named)
  Remarked, when I bade him farewell –'
'Oh, skip your dear uncle!' the Bellman exclaimed,
  As he angrily tingled his bell.

'He remarked to me then,' said that mildest of men,
  ' "If your Snark be a Snark, that is right:
Fetch it home by all means – you may serve it with greens,
  And it's handy for striking a light.

' "You may seek it with thimbles – and seek it with care;
  You may hunt it with forks and hope;
You may threaten its life with a railway-share;
  You may charm it with smiles and soap –" '

('That's exactly the method,' the Bellman bold
  In a hasty parenthesis cried,
'That's exactly the way I have always been told
  That the capture of Snarks should be tried!')

' "But oh, beamish nephew, beware of the day,
  If your Snark be a Boojum! For then
You will softly and suddenly vanish away,
  And never be met with again!"

'It is this, it is this that oppresses my soul,
  When I think of my uncle's last words:
And my heart is like nothing so much as a bowl
  Brimming over with quivering curds!

'It is this, it is this –' 'We have had that before!'
  The Bellman indignantly cried.
And the Baker replied, 'Let me say it once more.
  It is this, it is this that I dread!

'I engage with the Snark – every night after dark –
    In a dreamy delirious fight:
I serve it with greens in those shadowy scenes,
    And I use it for stiking a light;

'But if ever I meet with a Boojum, that day,
    In a moment (of this I am sure),
I shall softly and suddenly vanish away –
    And the notion I cannot endure!'

Fit the Fourth

THE HUNTING

The Bellman looked uffish, and wrinkled his brow.
    'If only you'd spoken before!
It's excessively awkward to mention it now,
    With the Snark, so to speak, at the door!

'We should all of us grieve, as you well may believe,
    If you never were met with again –
But surely, my man, when the voyage began,
    You might have suggested it then?

'It's excessively awkward to mention it now –
    As I think I've already remarked.'
And the man they called 'Hi!' replied, with a sigh,
    'I informed you the day we embarked.

'You may charge me with murder – or want of sense –
    (We are all of us weak at times):
But the slightest approach to a false pretence
    Was never among my crimes!

'I said it in Hebrew – I said it in Dutch –
    I said it in German and Greek;
But I wholly forgot (and it vexes me much)
    That English is what you speak!'

"TO PURSUE IT WITH FORKS AND HOPE"

''Tis a pitiful tale,' said the Bellman, whose face
   Had grown longer at every word;
'But, now that you've stated the whole of your case,
   More debate would be simply absurd.

'The rest of my speech' (he explained to his men)
   'You shall hear when I've leisure to speak it.
But the Snark is at hand, let me tell you again!
   'Tis your glorious duty to seek it!

'To seek it with thimbles, to seek it with care;
   To pursue it with forks and hope;
To threaten its life with a railway-share;
   To charm it with smiles and soap!

'For the Snark's a peculiar creature, that won't
   Be caught in a commonplace way.
Do all that you know, and try all that you don't:
   'Not a chance must be wasted to-day!

'For England expects – I forbear to proceed:
   'Tis a maxim tremendous, but trite:
And you'd best be unpacking the things that you need
   To rig yourselves out for the fight.'

Then the Banker endorsed a blank cheque (which he crossed),
   And changed his loose silver for notes.
The Baker with care combed his whiskers and hair,
   And shook the dust out of his coats.

The Boots and the Broker were sharpening a spade –
   Each working the grindstone in turn;
But the Beaver went on making lace, and displayed
   No interest in the concern:

Though the Barrister tried to appeal to its pride,
   And vainly proceeded to cite
A number of cases, in which making laces
   Had been proved an infringement of right.

The maker of Bonnets ferociously planned
    A novel arrangement of bows:
While the Billiard-marker with quivering hand
    Was chalking the tip of his nose.

But the Butcher turned nervous, and dressed himself fine,
    With yellow kid gloves and a ruff –
Said he felt it exactly like going to dine,
    Which the Bellman declared was all 'stuff'.

'Introduce me, now there's a good fellow,' he said,
    'If we happen to meet it together!'
And the Bellman, sagaciously nodding his head,
    Said, 'That must depend on the weather.'

The Beaver went simply galumphing about,
    At seeing the Butcher so shy:
And even the Baker, though stupid and stout,
    Made an effort to wink with one eye.

'Be a man!' said the Bellman in wrath, as he heard
    The Butcher beginning to sob.
'Should we meet with a Jubjub, that desperate bird,
    We shall need all our strength for the job!'

Fit the Fifth

THE BEAVER'S LESSON

They sought it with thimbles, they sought it with care;
    They pursued it with forks and hope;
They threatened its life with a railway-share;
    They charmed it with smiles and soap.

Then the Butcher contrived an ingenious plan
    For making a separate sally;
And had fixed on a spot unfrequented by man,
    A dismal and desolate valley.

97

But the very same plan to the Beaver occurred:
    It had chosen the very same place;
Yet neither betrayed, by a sign or a word,
    The disgust that appeared in his face.

Each thought he was thinking of nothing but 'Snark'
    And the glorious work of the day;
And each tried to pretend that he did not remark
    That the other was going that way.

But the valley grew narrow and narrower still,
    And the evening got darker and colder,
Till (merely from nervousness, not from goodwill)
    They marched along shoulder to shoulder.

Then a scream, shrill and high, rent the shuddering sky,
    And they knew that some danger was near:
The Beaver turned pale to the tip of its tail,
    And even the Butcher felt queer.

He thought of his childhood, left far behind –
    That blissful and innocent state –
The sound so exactly recalled to his mind
    A pencil that squeaks on a slate!

''Tis the voice of the Jubjub!' he suddenly cried.
    (This man, that they used to call 'Dunce'.)
'As the Bellman would tell you,' he added with pride,
    'I have uttered that sentiment once.

''Tis the note of the Jubjub! Keep count, I entreat;
    You will find I have told it you twice.
'Tis the song of the Jubjub! The proof is complete,
    If only I've stated it thrice.'

The Beaver had counted with scrupulous care,
    Attending to every word:
But it fairly lost heart, and outgrabe in despair,
    When the third repetition occurred.

THE BEAVER BROUGHT PAPER, PORTFOLIO, PENS

It felt that, in spite of all possible pains,
    It had somehow contrived to lose count,
And the only thing now was to rack its poor brains
    By reckoning up the amount.

'Two added to one – if that could but be done,'
    It said, 'with one's fingers and thumbs!'
Recollecting with tears how, in earlier years,
    It had taken no pains with its sums.

'The thing must be done,' said the Butcher, 'I think.
    The thing must be done, I am sure.
The thing shall be done! Bring me paper and ink,
    The best there is time to procure.'

The Beaver brought paper, portfolio, pens,
    And ink in unfailing supplies:
While strange creepy creatures came out of their dens,
    And watched them with wondering eyes.

So engrossed was the Butcher, he heeded them not,
    As he wrote with a pen in each hand,
And explained all the while in a popular style
    Which the Beaver could well understand.

'Taking Three as the subject to reason about –
    A convenient number to state –
We add Seven, and Ten, and then multiply out
    By One Thousand diminished by Eight.

'The result we proceed to divide, as you see,
    By Nine Hundred and Ninety and Two:
Then subtract Seventeen, and the answer must be
    Exactly and perfectly true.

'The method employed I would gladly explain,
    While I have it so clear in my head,
If I had but the time and you had but the brain –
    But much yet remains to be said.

'In one moment I've seen what has hitherto been
    Enveloped in absolute mystery,
And without extra charge I will give you at large
    A Lesson in Natural History.'

In his genial way he proceeded to say
    (Forgetting all laws of propriety,
And that giving instruction, without introduction,
    Would have caused quite a thrill in Society),

'As to temper the Jubjub's a desperate bird,
    Since it lives in perpetual passion:
Its taste in costume is entirely absurd –
    It is ages ahead of the fashion:

'But it knows any friend it has met once before:
    It never will look at a bribe:
And in charity-meetings it stands at the door,
    And collects – though it does not subscribe.

'Its flavour when cooked is more exquisite far
    Than mutton, or oysters, or eggs:
(Some think it keeps best in an ivory jar,
    And some, in mahogany kegs):

'You boil it in sawdust: you salt it in glue:
    'You condense it with locusts and tape:
Still keeping one principal object in view –
    To preserve its symmetrical shape.'

The Butcher would gladly have talked till next day,
    But he felt that the Lesson must end,
And he wept with delight in attempting to say
    He considered the Beaver his friend.

While the Beaver confessed, with affectionate looks
    More eloquent even than tears,
It had learnt in ten minutes far more than all books
    Would have taught it in seventy years.

They returned hand-in-hand, and the Bellman, unmanned
   (For a moment) with noble emotion,
Said, 'This amply repays all the wearisome days
   We have spent on the billowy ocean!'

Such friends, as the Beaver and Butcher became,
   Have seldom if ever been known;
In winter or summer, 'twas always the same –
   You could never meet either alone.

And when quarrels rose – as one frequently finds
   Quarrels will, spite of every endeavour –
The song of the Jubjub recurred to their minds,
   And cemented their friendship for ever!

Fit the Sixth

THE BARRISTER'S DREAM

They sought it with thimbles, they sought it with care;
   They pursued it with forks and hope;
They threatened its life with a railway-share;
   They charmed it with smiles and soap.

But the Barrister, weary of proving in vain
   That the Beaver's lace-making was wrong,
Fell asleep, and in dreams saw the creature quite plain
   That his fancy had dwelt on so long.

He dreamed that he stood in a shadowy Court,
   Where the Snark, with a glass in its eye,
Dressed in gown, bands, and wig, was defending a pig
   On the charge of deserting its sty.

The Witnesses proved, without error or flaw,
   That the sty was deserted when found:
And the Judge kept explaining the state of the law
   In a soft under-current of sound.

"YOU MUST KNOW——" SAID THE JUDGE: BUT THE SNARK EXCLAIMED, "FUDGE!"

The indictment had never been clearly expressed,
    And it seemed that the Snark had begun,
And had spoken three hours, before any one guessed
    What the pig was supposed to have done.

The Jury had each formed a different view
    (Long before the indictment was read),
And they all spoke at once, so that none of them knew
    One word that the others had said.

'You must know –' said the Judge: but the Snark exclaimed, 'Fudge!
    That statute is obsolete quite!
Let me tell you, my friends, the whole question depends
    On an ancient manorial right.

'In the matter of Treason the pig would appear
    To have aided, but scarcely abetted:
While the charge of Insolvency fails, it is clear,
    If you grant the plea "never indebted".

'The fact of Desertion I will not dispute:
    But its guilt, as I trust, is removed
(So far as relates to the costs of this suit)
    By the Alibi which has been proved.

'My poor client's fate now depends on your votes.'
    Here the speaker sat down in his place,
And directed the Judge to refer to his notes
    And briefly to sum up the case.

But the Judge said he never had summed up before;
    So the Snark undertook it instead,
And summed it so well that it came to far more
    Than the Witnesses ever had said!

When the verdict was called for, the Jury declined,
    As the word was so puzzling to spell;
But they ventured to hope that the Snark wouldn't mind
    Undertaking that duty as well.

So the Snark found the verdict, although, as it owned,
　　It was spent with the toils of the day:
When it said the word 'GUILTY!' the Jury all groaned,
　　And some of them fainted away.

Then the Snark pronounced sentence, the Judge being quite
　　Too nervous to utter a word:
When it rose to its feet, there was silence like night,
　　And the fall of a pin might be heard.

'Transportation for life' was the sentence it gave,
　　'And *then* to be fined forty pound.'
The Jury all cheered, though the Judge said he feared
　　That the phrase was not legally sound.

But their wild exultation was suddenly checked
　　When the jailer informed them, with tears,
Such a sentence would have not the slightest effect,
　　As the pig had been dead for some years.

The Judge left the Court, looking deeply disgusted:
　　But the Snark, though a little aghast,
As the lawyer to whom the defence was intrusted,
　　Went bellowing on to the last.

Thus the Barrister dreamed, while the bellowing seemed
　　To grow every moment more clear:
Till he woke to the knell of a furious bell,
　　Which the Bellman rang close at his ear.

Fit the Seventh

THE BANKER'S FATE

They sought it with thimbles, they sought it with care;
　　They pursued it with forks and hope;
They threatened its life with a railway-share;
　　They charmed it with smiles and soap.

SO GREAT WAS HIS FRIGHT THAT HIS WAISTCOAT TURNED WHITE

And the Banker, inspired with a courage so new
    It was matter for general remark,
Rushed madly ahead and was lost to their view
    In his zeal to discover the Snark.

But while he was seeking with thimbles and care,
    A Bandersnatch swiftly drew nigh
And grabbed at the Banker, who shrieked in despair,
    For he knew it was useless to fly.

He offered large discount – he offered a cheque
    (Drawn 'to bearer') for seven-pounds-ten:
But the Bandersnatch merely extended its neck
    And grabbed at the Banker again.

Without rest or pause – while those frumious jaws
    Went savagely snapping around –
He skipped and he hopped, and he floundered and flopped,
    Till fainting he fell to the ground.

The Bandersnatch fled as the others appeared:
    Led on by that fear-stricken yell:
And the Bellman remarked, 'It is just as I feared!'
    And solemnly tolled on his bell.

He was black in the face, and they scarcely could trace
    The least likeness to what he had been:
While so great was his fright that his waistcoat turned white –
    A wonderful thing to be seen!

To the horror of all who were present that day,
    He uprose in full evening dress,
And with senseless grimaces endeavoured to say
    What his tongue could no longer express.

Down he sank in a chair – ran his hands through his hair –
    And chanted in mimsiest tones
Words whose utter inanity proved his insanity,
    While he rattled a couple of bones.

'Leave him here to his fate – it is getting so late!'
    The Bellman exclaimed in a fright.
'We have lost half the day. Any further delay,
    And we shan't catch a Snark before night!'

Fit the Eighth

THE VANISHING

They sought it with thimbles, they sought it with care;
    They pursued it with forks and hope;
They threatened its life with a railway-share;
    They charmed it with smiles and soap.

They shuddered to think that the chase might fail,
    And the Beaver, excited at last,
Went bounding along on the tip of its tail,
    For the daylight was nearly past.

'There is Thingumbob shouting!' the Bellman said.
    'He is shouting like mad, only hark!
He is waving his hands, he is wagging his head,
    He has certainly found a Snark!'

They gazed in delight, while the Butcher exclaimed,
    'He was always a desperate wag!'
They beheld him – their Baker – their hero unnamed –
    On the top of a neighbouring crag,

Erect and sublime, for one moment of time.
    In the next, that wild figure they saw
(As if stung by a spasm) plunge into a chasm,
    While they waited and listened in awe.

'It's a Snark!' was the sound that first came to their ears,
    And seemed almost too good to be true.
Then followed a torrent of laughter and cheers:
    Then the ominous words, 'It's a Boo–'

THEN, SILENCE

Then, silence. Some fancied they heard in the air
    A weary and wandering sigh
That sounded like '–jum!' but the others declare
    It was only a breeze that went by.

They hunted till darkness came on, but they found
    Not a button, or feather, or mark,
By which they could tell that they stood on the ground
    Where the Baker had met with the Snark.

In the midst of the word he was trying to say,
    In the midst of his laughter and glee,
He had softly and suddenly vanished away –
    For the Snark *was* a Boojum, you see.

The Mad Gardener's Song

He thought he saw an Elephant
    That practised on a fife:
He looked again, and found it was
    A letter from his wife.
'At length I realise,' he said,
    'The bitterness of Life!'

He thought he saw a Buffalo
    Upon the chimney-piece:
He looked again, and found it was
    His Sister's Husband's Niece.
'Unless you leave this house,' he said,
    'I'll send for the Police!'

He thought he saw a Rattlesnake
   That questioned him in Greek:
He looked again, and found it was
   The Middle of Next Week.
'The one thing I regret,' he said,
   'Is that it cannot speak!'

He thought he saw a Banker's Clerk
   Descending from the bus:
He looked again, and found it was
   A Hippopotamus:
'If this should stay to dine,' he said,
   'There won't be much for us!'

He thought he saw a Kangaroo
   That worked a coffee-mill:
He looked again, and found it was
   A Vegetable-Pill.
'Were I to swallow this,' he said,
   'I should be very ill!'

He thought he saw a Coach-and-Four
   That stood beside his bed:
He looked again, and found it was
   A Bear without a Head.
'Poor thing,' he said, 'poor silly thing!
   It's waiting to be fed!'

He thought he saw an Albatross
   That fluttered round the lamp:
He looked again, and found it was
   A Penny-Postage-Stamp.
'You'd best be getting home,' he said:
   'The nights are very damp!'

He thought he saw a Garden-Door
   That opened with a key:
He looked again, and found it was

A Double Rule of Three:
'And all its mystery,' he said,
  'Is clear as day to me!'

He thought he saw an Argument
    That proved he was the Pope:
He looked again, and found it was
    A Bar of Mottled Soap.
'A fact so dread,' he faintly said,
    'Extinguishes all hope!'

The Three Badgers

There be three Badgers on a mossy stone
    Beside a dark and covered way:
Each dreams himself a monarch on his throne,
    And so they stay and stay –
Though their old Father languishes alone,
    They stay, and stay, and stay.

There be three Herrings loitering around,
    Longing to share that mossy seat:
Each Herring tries to sing what she has found
    That makes Life seem so sweet.
Thus, with a grating and uncertain sound,
    They bleat, and bleat, and bleat.

The Mother-Herring, on the salt sea-wave,
    Sought vainly for her absent ones:
The Father-Badger, writhing in a cave,
    Shrieked out 'Return, my sons!
You shall have buns,' he shrieked, 'if you'll behave!
    Yea, buns, and buns, and buns!'

'I fear,' said she, 'your sons have gone astray.
  My daughters left me while I slept.'
'Yes 'm,' the Badger said: 'it's as you say.
    'They should be better kept.'
Thus the poor parents talked the time away,
    And wept, and wept, and wept.

'Oh, dear beyond our dearest dreams,
Fairer than all that fairest seems!
To feast the rosy hours away,
To revel in a roundelay!
    How blest would be
    A life so free –
Ipwergis-Pudding to consume,
And drink the subtle Azzigoom!

'And if, in other days and hours,
Mid other fluffs and other flowers,
The choice were given me how to dine –
"Name what thou wilt: it shall be thine!"
    Oh, then I see
    The life for me –
Ipwergis-Pudding to consume,
And drink the subtle Azzigoom!'

The Badgers did not care to talk to Fish:
  They did not dote on Herrings' songs:
They never had experienced the dish
    To which that name belongs:
'And oh, to pinch their tails,' (this was their wish,)
    'With tongs, yea, tongs, and tongs!'

'And are not these the Fish,' the Eldest sighed,
  'Whose Mother dwells beneath the foam?'
'They *are* the Fish!' the Second one replied.
    'And they have left their home!'
'Oh, wicked Fish,' the Youngest Badger cried,
    'To roam, yea, roam, and roam!'

113

Gently the Badgers trotted to the shore –
     The sandy shore that fringed the bay:
Each in his mouth a living Herring bore –
          Those aged ones waxed gay:
Clear rang their voices through the ocean's roar,
          'Hooray, hooray, hooray!'

The King-Fisher Song

King Fisher courted Lady Bird –
Sing Beans, sing Bones, sing Butterflies!
     'Find me my match,' he said,
     'With such a noble head –
With such a beard, as white as curd –
     With such expressive eyes!'

'Yet pins have heads,' said Lady Bird –
Sing Prunes, sing Prawns, sing Primrose-Hill!
     'And, where you stick them in,
     They stay, and thus a pin
Is very much to be preferred
     To one that's never still!'

'Oysters have beards,' said Lady Bird –
Sing Flies, sing Frogs, sing Fiddle-strings!
     'I love them, for I know
     They never chatter so:
They would not say one single word –
     Not if you crowned them Kings!'

'Needles have eyes,' said Lady Bird –
Sing Cats, sing Corks, sing Cowslip-tea!
     'And they are sharp – just what
     Your Majesty is *not*:
So get you gone – 'tis too absurd
     To come a-courting *me*!'

114

The Pig-Tale

Little Birds are dining
        Warily and well
        Hid in mossy cell:
Hid, I say, by waiters
Gorgeous in their gaiters –
        I've a Tale to tell.

Little Birds are feeding
        Justices with jam,
        Rich in frizzled ham:
Rich, I say, in oysters
Haunting shady cloisters –
        That is what I am.

Little Birds are teaching
        Tigresses to smile,
        Innocent of guile:
Smile, I say, not smirkle –
Mouth a semicircle,
        That's the proper style!

Little Birds are sleeping
        All among the pins,
        Where the loser wins:
Where, I say, he sneezes,
When and how he pleases –
        So the Tale begins.

There was a Pig that sat alone
    Beside a ruined Pump:
By day and night he made his moan –
It would have stirred a heart of stone
To see him wring his hoofs and groan,
    Because he could not jump.

A certain Camel heard him shout –
   A Camel with a hump.
'Oh, is it Grief, or is it Gout?
What is this bellowing about?'
That Pig replied, with quivering snout,
   'Because I cannot jump!'

That Camel scanned him, dreamy-eyed.
   'Methinks you are too plump.
I never knew a Pig so wide –
That wobbled so from side to side –
Who could, however much he tried,
   Do such a thing as *jump*!

'Yet mark those trees, two miles away,
   All clustered in a clump:
If you could trot there twice a day,
Nor ever pause for rest or play,
In the far future – Who can say? –
   You may be fit to jump.'

That Camel passed, and left him there
   Beside the ruined Pump.
Oh, horrid was that Pig's despair!
His shrieks of anguish filled the air.
He wrung his hoofs, he rent his hair,
   Because he could not jump.

There was a Frog that wandered by –
   A sleek and shining lump:
Inspected him with fishy eye,
And said, 'O Pig, what makes you cry?'
And bitter was that Pig's reply,
   'Because I cannot jump!'

That Frog he grinned a grin of glee,
   And hit his chest a thump.
'O Pig,' he said, 'be ruled by me,

116

And you shall see what you shall see.
This minute, for a trifling fee,
  I'll teach you how to jump!

'You may be faint from many a fall,
  And bruised by many a bump:
But, if you persevere through all,
And practise first on something small,
Concluding with a ten-foot wall,
  You'll find that you *can* jump!'

That Pig looked up with joyful start:
  'Oh, Frog, you *are* a trump!
Your words have healed my inward smart –
Come, name your fee and do your part:
Bring comfort to a broken heart,
  By teaching me to jump!'

'My fee shall be a mutton-chop,
  My goal this ruined Pump.
Observe with what an airy flop
I plant myself upon the top!
Now bend your knees and take a hop,
  For that's the way to jump!'

Uprose that Pig, and rushed, full whack,
  Against the ruined Pump:
Rolled over like an empty sack,
And settled down upon his back,
While all his bones at once went 'Crack!'
  It was a fatal jump.

> *Little Birds are writing*
> *Interesting books,*
> *To be read by cooks:*
> *Read, I say, not roasted –*
> *Letterpress, when toasted,*
> *Loses its good looks.*

117

Little Birds are playing
    Bagpipes on the shore,
    Where the tourists snore:
'Thanks!' they cry. ''Tis thrilling
Take, oh, take this shilling!
    Let us have no more!'

Little Birds are bathing
    Crocodiles in cream,
    Like a happy dream:
Like, but not so lasting –
Crocodiles, when fasting,
    Are not all they seem!

That Camel passed, as day grew dim
  Around the ruined Pump.
'O broken heart! O broken limb!
It needs,' that Camel said to him,
'Something more fairy-like and slim,
  To execute a jump!'

That Pig lay still as any stone,
  And could not stir a stump:
Nor ever, if the truth were known,
Was he again observed to moan,
Nor ever wring his hoofs and groan,
  Because he could not jump.

That Frog made no remark, for he
  Was dismal as a dump:
He knew the consequence must be
That he would never get his fee –
And still he sits, in miserie,
  Upon that ruined Pump!

Little Birds are choking
    Baronets with bun,
    Taught to fire a gun:

Taught, I say, to splinter
Salmon in the winter –
    Merely for the fun.

Little Birds are hiding
    Crimes in carpet-bags,
    Blessed by happy stags:
Blessed, I say, though beaten –
Since our friends are eaten
    When the memory flags.

Little Birds are tasting
    Gratitude and gold,
    Pale with sudden cold:
Pale, I say, and wrinkled –
When the bells have tinkled,
    And the Tale is told.

'Jabberwocky' – Humpty Dumpty Explains

'You seem very clever at explaining words, Sir,' said Alice. 'Would you kindly tell me the meaning of the poem called "Jabberwocky"?'

'Let's hear it,' said Humpty Dumpty. 'I can explain all the poems that ever were invented – and a good many that haven't been invented just yet.'

This sounded very hopeful, so Alice repeated the first verse:

> *'Twas brillig, and the slithy toves*
> *Did gyre and gimble in the wabe:*
> *All mimsy were the borogoves,*
> *And the mome raths outgrabe.'*

'That's enough to begin with,' Humpty Dumpty interrupted: 'there are plenty of hard words there. "*Brillig*" means four o'clock in the afternoon – the time when you begin *broiling* things for dinner.'

'That'll do very well,' said Alice: 'and "*slithy*"?'

'Well, "*slithy*" means "lithe and slimy". "Lithe" is the same as "active". You see it's like a portmanteau – there are two meanings packed up into one word.'

'I see it now,' Alice remarked thoughtfully: 'and what are "*toves*"?'

'Well, "*toves*" are something like badgers – they're something like lizards – and they're something like corkscrews."

'They must be very curious-looking creatures.'

'They are that,' said Humpty Dumpty; 'also they make their nests under sun-dials – also they live on cheese.'

'And what's to "*gyre*" and to "*gimble*"?'

'To "*gyre*" is to go round and round like a gyroscope. To "*gimble*" is to make holes like a gimlet.'

'And "*the wabe*" is the grass-plot round a sun-dial, I suppose?' said Alice, surprised at her own ingenuity.

'Of course it is. It's called "*wabe*" you know, because it goes a long way before it, and a long way behind it –'

'And a long way beyond it on each side,' Alice added.

'Exactly so. Well then, "*mimsy*" is "flimsy and miserable"

(there's another portmanteau for you). And a *"borogove"* is a thin shabby-looking bird with its feathers sticking out all round – something like a live mop.'

'And then *"mome raths"*?' said Alice. 'I'm afraid I'm giving you a great deal of trouble.'

'Well, a *"rath"* is a sort of green pig: but *"mome"* I'm not certain about. I think it's short for "from home" – meaning that they'd lost their way, you know.'

'And what does *"outgrabe"* mean?'

'Well, *"outgrabing"* is something between bellowing and whistling, with a kind of sneeze in the middle: however, you'll hear it done, maybe – down in the wood yonder – and, when you've once heard it, you'll be *quite* content. Who's been repeating all that hard stuff to you?'

'I read it in a book,' said Alice. 'But I *had* some poetry repeated to me much easier than that, by – Tweedledee, I think it was.'

'As to poetry, you know,' said Humpty Dumpty, stretching out one of his great hands, '*I* can repeat poetry as well as other folk, if it comes to that –'

'Oh, it needn't come to that!' Alice hastily said, hoping to keep him from beginning.

– from *Alice Through the Looking Glass*
Chapter VI

Index of first lines